Dangerous Opportunity: Making Change Work

SECOND EDITION

Dangerous Opportunity: Making Change Work

SECOND EDITION

Chris Musselwhite, Ed.D.
with Randell Jones, MBA

To order additional copies of this book, contact:
Discovery Learning, Inc.
336.272.9530
www.discoverylearning.com
21444

Contents

List of Figures

Acknowledgments

There are many people to thank for helping to make this book a reality. First, I must acknowledge two organizations. The W.K. Kellogg Foundation supported and encouraged the experiences that made the early research on effective change agents possible. Through its Kellogg National Leadership Development Program, the Kellogg Foundation expanded my view of the world as well as what I was capable of doing and being. I must also acknowledge the Center for Creative Leadership for providing the arena for exploring the early concepts of change style preferences with real managers who faced real problems.

There are too many individuals to acknowledge everyone, but a few do bear mentioning for their support, ideas and encouragement. A special thanks in no special order goes to Robyn Ingram, Cheryl DeCiantis, Sandra Daley, Diana Chapman Walsh, Nancy Snyderman, Stan Gryskiewicz, James Selman, Don Hanna, Rick Foster, Bill Neale, Don deBethizy, Keith Caver, Carl Bryant, and Kathleen Ponder.

And finally a big thanks to Quinn Dalton, the people of King's English, and Bonnie Parks for all their encouragement, editorial assistance, and attention to detail.

Part One

Danger and Opportunity

Together, these characters form the Mandarin Chinese word for "crisis."

Introduction

Change is a natural force, a constant and continuing phenomenon. It may come in regular, predictable cycles such as the changing of the seasons or the onset of the monsoons. It may erupt abruptly and unexpectedly, as do tornados and earthquakes. It may develop as an anticipated, but highly unpredictable, phenomenon such as a hurricane. Change can create a crisis and change may be the solution to a crisis. In our personal and work lives we experience corresponding changes—births, deaths, divorce, moves, downsizing, promotions, mergers, shifting markets and more.

Just as the nature of change is varied, so are human responses and reactions to change. Some people are confused, confounded and compromised by the changes they experience and the unpredictability of circumstances that confront them. Others find the prospect of uncertainty invigorating and relish finding new and different situations that promise opportunities for excitement and exploration.

Two people experiencing the same event may describe it quite differently. What to one person is insignificant or even exciting may be a major crisis to another. It is that perspective of change that may have led the ancient Chinese to create the character for "crisis" as a combination of the characters for both "danger" and "opportunity." So it is that people relate to change in unique, varied and sometimes unpredictable ways.

Background

The Change Style Preferences presented in this book are measured by the Change Style Indicator®, a self-assessment instrument. The Change Style Indicator model and assessment tool were conceived and developed over a 10-year period by Discovery Learning, Inc. The Change Style Indicator has been used with over 150,000 people, and Discovery Learning maintains a constantly growing database which currently has over 20,000 respondents. The database is segmented to show differences by profession, industry, gender, and Myers-Briggs Type. Current Change Style Indicator norms are available on the Discovery Learning Web site at *www.discoverylearning.com*.

Two documents describe the development and validation of the Change Style Indicator. These are *Change Style Indicator: Research and Development Report* and Chapter Five, "Research," of the *Change Style Indicator Facilitator Guide*. Both documents are available from Discovery Learning, Inc.

This book describes the three Change Style Preferences in action in organizations and offers prescriptive strategies for improved effectiveness. To obtain a copy of the Change Style Indicator, contact Discovery Learning, Inc. at 336.272.9530 or via email: *info@discoverylearning.com*. Change Style Indicator is available in a self-scored format and online.

What This Book Does

This book, with its presentation of theory and data, empirical truth, anecdotal evidence and opinion:

- Addresses the interests of individuals—leaders, executives, managers—to better understand the human relationship to change.

- Introduces two simple but powerful models that enable you to see yourself and others more clearly in relationship to change.
- Enables you to understand how this new knowledge can empower you to manage groups and organizations more effectively through situations requiring change.
- Helps you understand disagreements with others in changing situations.
- Demonstrates how to create the powerful advantage of collaboration by directing collective energy into creating and producing rather than blaming, defending and fighting.

Chapter 1

CHANGE—DANGER OR OPPORTUNITY?

A New View of Change

Much has been written, but little is actually understood about the human relationship to change. Change is so much a part of our human experience, that to address it effectively, the exploration must be framed in terms of the human psyche and our social/cultural milieu. We are, after all, products of the cultures in which we grow and live, and we know that different cultures, even subcultures, have differing interpretations of similar phenomena. Consider time, personal space, authority, family and pride, to name a few. Much of the current debate about change revolves around simplistic ideologies that label some people as "pro-change" and others as "change resistors." Predictably, the "pro-change" forces are seen as the good guys and the resistors are the enemies of progress.

One problem with this ideology is that the people who frame these arguments have their own unique attitudes, beliefs and preferences—their personal mind-sets about change. The fact that the pro-change person may lead his/her organization into a disaster or that the resistor may present objections for very sound reasons is often ignored in the discourse. In the current debate, personal change preferences are often confused with change competency.

The Age Old Question—Evolution vs. Revolution

People are not just victims of change, responding to events beyond their control. They are also initiators of change, rearranging their surroundings and putting into play new situations, relationships and behaviors. As initiators of change, some people prefer an evolutionary approach. They want to make gradual, incremental changes in what they know works, so they can create something that works better with the least amount of disruption. Others want to create something that is radically different from anything that has existed before. Their intuition may be the only supporting evidence that it will work, but they are willing to accept the risk. These people are the change revolutionaries.

Both approaches have produced great successes. In 1776, 13 colonies decided to make a radical change based on an emerging belief that people should be free to govern themselves. To gain this freedom required six years of unconventional warfare against the strongest empire in the world. By contrast, it is reported that Thomas Edison conducted over 10,000 experiments in his effort to create the incandescent light bulb. He kept meticulous records and would make slight alterations with each new experiment.

Neither approach is right or wrong; neither is good or bad. Nevertheless, as a function of personality, individuals tend to prefer one approach over the other. Along with this broad spectrum of preference for change comes a host of challenges. On the personal level, misunderstandings, tensions, disagreements, competition and other interpersonal frictions can stymie the efforts of an individual or group.

It's Not the Change, It's the People

At the organizational and social level, norms and beliefs that frame acceptable behavior, ethics, and group identity have great impact on the individual and collective mind-set through which change is perceived and interpreted. Consequently, the phenomenon of "change" does not need managing as much as do the people involved with it. Understanding and acceptance of the ways people frame change is critical to the effectiveness and success of organizational change projects. Building that understanding and achieving that acceptance are two of the most important and pressing challenges facing leaders today.

Living Change

Change as a process is pervasive in its effect on human lives. People can create it, anticipate it, observe it and plan it. They can wish it hadn't happened or that it had worked out its effects some other way. They can praise it, curse it and ignore it, but they can't hold it back. It is the responsibility of leaders and organizations to embrace effective change—change that works for the common good of organizations, communities and families, not change that gratifies the beliefs and personal preferences of individuals. For some the challenge will be to stretch their comfort level with uncertainty and chaos; for others it will be to slow down and reflect. For some the challenge will be to respect past and current policies; for others it will be to embrace new ideas. For some the challenge will be to question new ideas. For everyone, the challenge will be to know your own Change Style Preferences, both strengths and weaknesses, and to respect the preferences of others as they play out in the form of differing ideas, opinions and behaviors. This is the path to building more organic organizations that "live" change rather than organizations that must be changed.

Chapter 2

CHANGING CONDITIONS

Leadership, Change Styles and Extreme Risk

In This Chapter

To prepare to introduce the concept of Change Styles, we've included a powerful story of two individuals with distinctly different leadership styles. The story shows how they approached a dangerous and uncertain situation, and how they experienced and responded to rapidly changing circumstances.

This incident was a terrible tragedy. The events as related here are based on the written accounts of others and are used to illustrate the different approaches which leaders take in uncertain and risky situations. The authors do not intend to imply any fault with regard to the decisions made or the actions taken by the individuals represented in this story. The published accounts of this disaster differ significantly in perspectives and interpretations of this tragedy. It was a tragic experience, but like so much of human history, important lessons can be learned by reflecting on events of the past.

By the Book

Rob Hall was a climber's climber. Within a seven-month period in 1990, he had climbed the highest mountain on each of the seven continents. A New Zealand mountaineer in the tradition of Sir Edmund Hillary, in six years he had put 39 people atop Mt. Everest, more than any other guide. In 1996, he was planning to extend his achievement with the success of another expedition. Hall's reputation was legendary and his expeditions were popular with many amateur climbers who were willing to pay a fee on the order of $65,000 to be led to the summit of Mt. Everest. He advertised a 100 percent success rate until 1995 when he forced all his clients to turn around a few hundred feet short of the summit because of deep snow, slow progress and changing conditions. To have continued, he believed, was too great a risk. It would have been inconsistent with the careful and respectful style that was the hallmark of Rob Hall's approach to Mt. Everest. But, in a business environment growing more competitive by the month, Hall was determined to make his next climb in the spring of 1996 a success.

Hall was meticulous in his preparations for every climb. He looked after minute details—the health of his Sherpas, the efficiency of his solar-powered electrical system and the sharpness of his clients' crampons (devices with sharpened metal points attached to climbers' boots for ice climbing). He was an expert quartermaster and organizer of the camps staged at progressively higher elevations used in ascending to the summit. At the base camp from which all teams began the ascent, he earned the respect of the other guides who often asked for his advice. His camp became the *de facto* seat of government for all climbers.

At the beginning of the 1996 climbing season[1] 16 teams and 300-plus people representing at least 22 nationalities were crowded into the Everest base camp. Hall organized the effort to schedule ascents for these competing teams to avoid a dangerous bottleneck of climbers at the summit.

According to Hall, "With enough determination any bloody idiot can get up this hill. The trick is to get back down alive" (Krakauer, 1999, p. 153). He knew the dangers of climbing in "the death zone" where the environment—at the cruising altitude of commercial airlines—is incompatible with human life. He knew the risks of pulmonary and cerebral edema, both brought on by long-term exposure to high altitudes. He knew the threat of afternoon storms and religiously followed a strict timetable for ascending and descending the peak to reduce the risk of getting caught.

His plan was carefully arranged. The final ascent for a noontime summit would start at midnight. Four Sherpas would leave 90 minutes earlier to affix ropes at Hillary Step to be in place when the team arrived.[2] And, as always, all climbers would turn around and begin descending by 2:00 P.M., regardless. About this point, Hall was emphatic. He climbed with discipline. "My word will be absolute law, beyond appeal," he lectured at base camp. "If you don't like a particular decision I make, I'd be happy to discuss it with you afterwards, but not while we're on 'The Hill.'"

On the Fly

In 1996, an American competitor also arrived at the Everest base camp. Another well-respected mountaineer, Scott Fischer was vying for expedition business in America, a substantial part of Hall's clientele. Fischer had climbed Everest only once, in 1994 (on his fourth attempt), and had never guided an ascent. He was new to the commercial climbing business and his enterprise was marginally financed. Fischer did not enjoy Hall's international reputation and he desperately needed a successful ascent to attract more clients. One of his customers was a New York socialite with little climbing experience. She had brought along a satellite dish from which to uplink her daily reports about the ascent. This visibility would bring Fischer's team the publicity his *Mountain Madness* enterprise needed.

Fischer had a relentlessly upbeat attitude. Those who knew him well said he had manic energy and was a gregarious person known for his "full-speed-ahead" ascents. Some climbers noted his success at employing a "make-it-up-as-you-go" climbing style. Others marveled that he had survived numerous mishaps. Fischer believed that climbing was a mental challenge. He told a potential client whom he was recruiting for his Everest expedition, "Hey, experience is overrated. It's not the altitude that's important, it's your attitude, bro . . . . We've got the 'Big E' figured out: We've built a yellow brick road to the summit" (Krakauer, 1999, p. 70). At the Everest base camp, Fischer told his team, "If you're bumming out, you're not going to get to the top. So long as we are up here, we might as well make a point of grooving" (Krakauer, p. 154).

Relying on his usually successful by-the-seat-of-the-pants style, Fischer had a loosely formulated plan for the ascent of Mt. Everest on summit day. He believed in giving his clients free reign to go up and down the mountain independently. Fischer's lead guide was a Russian climber, Anatoli Boukreev, known for his technical ability and experience in high-altitude climbing. His social skills were lacking (though some attribute that primarily to the language barrier), and he operated from a Russian ethic that the weak should not be coddled. Some people did not consider Boukreev to be a team player, and his critics were concerned that he did not watch out for his people.[3] His own account of the events that occurred on the deadliest day in Mount Everest history suggests that his natural strength and climbing expertise enabled him to perform acts of heroism (Boukreev & DeWalt, 1997).

May 10, 1996

At midnight on May 10, both Hall's and Fischer's teams were to begin the ascent together, along with a Taiwanese team. The teams staggered their departures to avoid a congestion of climbers on the route to the summit, especially at Hillary Step. Hall gave his team specific and clear instructions about the climb—what to expect, what to do in different situations and when to turn back. Fischer gave his team personal supplies and hypodermics, to self-administer in case of edema. Fischer encouraged his team by joking about their "invincibility." Hall required all his team to climb with oxygen. Fischer allowed his lead guide, Boukreev, to climb without oxygen.[4]

The teams arrived at Hillary Step to discover that the Sherpas had not been able to affix the ropes, thus delaying the climbers while the ropes were put in place. During the delay, other climbers ascending behind them were approaching the Hillary Step as well. Soon there would be a traffic jam of ascending climbers on this narrow one-way corridor. After mounting the Step, the climbers proceeded slowly and laboriously along the final ridge to the summit.

By now climbers were strung out along the mountain. Throughout the early afternoon climbers arrived and celebrated their summit in five minutes of victory at the top of the world. They then began their descent and the Hillary Step became congested with ascending and descending climbers. When 2:00 P.M. arrived, Hall and some lagging members of his team were not yet at the summit. Despite his history of disciplined climbing, Hall did not turn back as he had previously, but proceeded with one of his clients to the summit. They arrived at 4:00 P.M., late and exhausted.[5] Fischer had arrived at the summit at 3:40 P.M. He too was exhausted physically and mentally and suffering from a gastrointestinal problem that flared up when he was under stress.

As Hall and Fischer and the others were beginning their descent late in the day, they were surprised by a rogue storm blowing up the mountain. These were not unusual events, and the two o'clock turnaround time was established in part to respect the potential for these afternoon storms, which could arrive virtually unseen. The teams had scheduled their climbs during the short, recognized climbing season, but were now facing the terrifying prospect of being caught in the open on Mt. Everest in a raging storm.

Some of the climbers were separated from their parties. The snow was blinding and the subarctic cold was further numbing what little rational judgment remained after the constant battle with the effects of extreme altitude. A disaster loomed. A few climbers walked off the mountain, disappearing into the dark and the jagged, icy rocks thousands of feet below. Some lay down in the deepening snow never to get up again. Sadly, Fischer and Hall froze to death, though Hall somehow managed to survive the night on the mountain. In all, 10 people died in the storm. Though over 150 people have died attempting to climb Mt. Everest, May 10, 1996 was the deadliest single day in the history of the mountain.

Comparing Styles

One of the other nearby teams, not yet on the final assault, was led by David Breashears. An accomplished climber and cinematographer, he was the expedition leader for a team attempting to capture the ascent of Everest for an IMAX film. The IMAX team's ascent was interrupted by the disaster on May 10th, as they temporarily abandoned their project and participated in the rescue efforts. As a member of the international high-altitude climbing community, Breashears knew both Rob Hall and Scott Fischer, having climbed with both men on separate occasions. Breashears was present at an Everest base camp meeting attended by a representative from each climbing team to discuss ground rules, climbing sequence and other logistical issues. The following description of Fischer and Hall is from Breashears' book, *High Exposure*. This excerpt is a part of Breashears' description of this meeting.

"Scott and Rob made for an interesting contrast in styles. Rob was very analytical, precise and ran a tight operation. For him, his abilities and knowledge of the mountain were the key to success. Scott was much more freewheeling. His leadership style exhibited great faith in the human spirit, as if to say to clients, *I'm not going to hold your hand all the way, I'm not going to map it out for you, There's something in this experience for you to sort out on your own.* It was Scott's nature to leave a few bases uncovered" (Breashears, 1999, pp. 240-241).

Scott seemed to be aware of the potential consequences of his trusting style, yet he still chose to operate in his hands-off style as described by Breashears. "Scott pointed out that high on the mountain, where supplies and energy are limited, there was an increasing tendency for underequipped teams to 'borrow' crucial supplies. In his firm but laid-back way, Scott said, 'That's not right. If you put something on the mountain, it's yours.'"

Breashears reports a contrast in Hall's leadership style. "Then Rob delivered his own message. 'I don't mind being the mountain's policeman,' he said. 'I'm a great guy to have as a friend, but I'm a bad person to have as your enemy. If anyone leaves garbage on the mountain, even so much as one paper wrapper, you're going to have to answer to me.'"

In this story, as tragic as it was, two men demonstrate different attitudes, values and approaches to a difficult, dangerous and rapidly changing situation.

- Rob Hall was a disciplined planner. He was deliberate and organized. Experience had taught him what worked and what did not. He was cautious, but not fearful. His hallmark was preparation and he focused on details. He honored the traditions of those who preceded him and respected cultures and established practices wherever he visited.

- Scott Fischer was enthusiastic about climbing. He was driven by the goal of getting to the summit and was willing to use unorthodox strategies and techniques to get there. He may have appeared unorganized or undisciplined to some, but his experience had given him confidence in his ability to think on his feet and to overcome unforeseen barriers to achieve his goals. He was eager to take on new and unexplored challenges. He was willing to alter his plans as the situation changed. He trusted his own capacity to respond to changing circumstances and he assumed others were as willing and able as he to operate in this free-form, make-it-up-as-you-go style.

Hall and Fischer had distinctly different approaches to meeting the challenges of climbing Mt. Everest. Each had experienced previous success in using a preferred style. Yet, when confronted with the need to decide on a course of action in the face of changing conditions, each had to cope with different challenges.

- Fischer had not anticipated (and had no plan in place to deal with) the scenario that unfolded; it was not part of his plan. When the life-threatening challenge arose, Fischer had no time, no means, no framework, no experience and no energy to spontaneously craft a new plan.
- On the other hand, Hall had a well-prepared and tested plan in place to avoid just this situation, but he did not follow it. Perhaps at the moment, he gave greater credence to some other factor, such as his allegiance to a client or the new competitive pressures his company faced. In any event, he deviated from his tested plan in the most critical of situations.

The tragic story of Rob Hall and Scott Fischer, two highly skilled and experienced individuals, highlights two very different approaches to the same complex and fluid situation. It demonstrates remarkably well the elemental characteristics of two different Change Style Preferences, which are explained and developed in the following chapters. Their differences are captured in concepts like attention to detail, need for planning, relationship to rules, individual responsibility, and response to risk and the unexpected. If managing change is about anticipating the future, finding new directions, taking people to places they have never been before, planning for the unexpected and being responsible for the consequences, then the personality characteristics portrayed by Fischer and Hall can have considerable impact on how one leads change efforts. This story may be an extreme case; the usual consequences of responding to changing circumstances are not so dire. However, as any experienced leader knows, no change is without its dangers as well as its opportunities.

Notes

[1] The climbing season for the summit of Mount Everest is between the end of winter and the monsoons. For the summit, this may be limited to two or three weeks in the latter part of May. However, it may take five or six weeks to reach the Everest base camp.

[2] Hillary Step, named for Sir Edmund Hillary who, along with Sherpa Tensing Norgay, first reached the summit of Mount Everest in 1953, is a steep 40-foot high rocky cliff. It is the only place on the Southeast Ridge route that requires ropes and technical climbing skills. Because only one person can pass through the Hillary Step at a time (either going up or coming down), it can create a bottleneck for ascending and descending climbers.

[3] These accounts have been supported by other climbers. Boukreev died in 1997 in an avalanche while climbing on Annapurna on Christmas Day. Annapurna is the world's tenth-highest mountain.

4   Some climbers, including John Krakauer, author of *Into Thin Air,* and David Breashears, author of *High Exposure,* consider this an unconscionable choice. Climbing without oxygen at such altitudes is extremely risky. At the summit of Mount Everest the human body gets less than one-fourth the oxygen as at sea level. Climbing Mount Everest without supplemental oxygen is a challenge and not one, they believe, to be taken when one is responsible for the safety of less experienced climbers.

5   It remains unclear to those involved in these events why Hall violated his own strict rule for turning around. All agree that one's judgment and decision making are strongly impaired at high altitudes. Some speculate his choice was based on a sense of duty to one of his clients whom he had turned around the year before just short of the summit. Others suspect the business pressures of commercial climbing affected his decision to continue climbing beyond 2:00 P.M.

Chapter 3

A MATTER OF PREFERENCE

Introducing Conservers, Pragmatists and Originators

In This Chapter

How people deal with change—both creating it and responding to it—is a function of identifiable preferences. Whether they see change as a danger, a challenge or an opportunity, people have individual preferences that reflect, at the most basic level, their relationship to structure, rules and authority.

In this chapter we will:

- Introduce the concept of Change Styles.[1]
- Define the Conserver, Pragmatist and Originator Change Style Preferences.
- Provide detailed characteristics for each Change Style.

Dangerous Opportunity takes a more systemic view of change. Change is viewed on a continuum with the preferences of Rob Hall, the evolutionary incrementalist, defining one end of the continuum and Scott Fischer, the revolutionary radical, defining the other. Between the evolutionist and revolutionist is the situationalist. Situationalists are inclined to approach change from a more pragmatic, problem-solving approach, focusing attention more on attaining workable outcomes. The Change Style Preference Model described in this book defines these Change Style Preferences as Conservers, Pragmatists and Originators.

Introducing Conservers, Pragmatists and Originators

For ages, debates have existed over the best way to approach change. In various arenas, from politics to economics, from business to education, debates have argued evolution vs. revolution, incrementalism vs. innovation, reform vs. reinvention, and total quality management vs. reengineering. Often these debates have had an either/or quality; one approach is right and the other is wrong. Such a framework for change frequently produces conflict, misunderstanding, strong-arming and missed opportunities . . . not the outcomes envisioned by the change initiators.

Conservers—The Evolutionists

Conservers are good at defining and clarifying current reality. Working together to build upon what is already working is the preferred path to change for a Conserver. Conservers prefer working within existing systems and structures (i.e., relationships, authority/reporting patterns, policies, processes and procedures) to create improvements. Peter Brabeck, the CEO of Nestlé, a Swiss company founded in 1866, epitomizes this style in the following statement. "Nestlé caters to billions of consumers around the world. In our business—food and drink—more perhaps than in others, we need a relationship of trust to be successful. Can anyone trust a company that reinvents itself every few years? Sure, we can act swiftly to change our products and our business methods if need be, and we can do our best to improve all aspects of our company each day. But we will never allow our value system, or our focus on quality and safety, to deteriorate. Trust is our most important asset. We must always defend it. That's why I think one of the main jobs of the leader is to determine what aspects of the company you want to keep. You have to be clear about why the company has been successful in the past and how you are going to keep those fundamentals from breaking down and disappearing" (Wetlaufer, 2001, pp. 114-115).

Conservers favor a "total quality management/continuous improvement" approach to organizational change. They may, in fact, see the need for substantial systemic change but prefer to make those changes gradually. Conservers want to keep the current system working smoothly and will resist decisions and efforts that they perceive will create chaos. Conservers will ask the hard questions of proposed change: How will this be better than what we have now? Why is the standard practice we have followed all this time no longer acceptable? Who will be affected by this proposed change? What are the political implications of the change? What will this cost? What is the return on investment? What is the loss in productivity and effectiveness to the organization resulting from these changes?

Used effectively, these questions are beneficial to any organization in change. Used ineffectively, they create the appearance of obstruction and foot-dragging as we will see in upcoming stories.

Pragmatists—The Situationalists

Pragmatists tend to focus on viable results—getting the job done—more so than on challenging or preserving existing structure. Pragmatists often see the merit in both an evolutionary and a revolutionary approach and are more motivated to find adequate and timely solutions to problems than to advance ideologies.

Dr. Eric Schmidt is the CEO and Chairman of Novell, Inc., a networking software maker founded in 1983. Taking the helm of Novell in 1997, Schmidt faced a daunting "turnaround." The company was in dire straits with Microsoft's Windows NT operating system competing aggressively for its market. In the face of this crisis, Schmidt describes his biggest challenge as retaining the smartest employees. His strategy is captured in his own words: "I've found that the best way to manage smart people is to let them self-organize so they can operate both inside and outside the management hierarchy. They report to a manager, but they also have the latitude to work on projects that interest them, regardless of whether they originate with their own manager. You tell them, 'Look, I don't know how to solve this problem, so why don't you throw yourself at it and figure it out? Take the time and resources you need, and get it right.' If they get frustrated and need to blow off steam, you invite them to talk with you directly—no go-betweens. At the same time, you discuss this new component of the person's work directly with his or her manager, and there are no reprisals when a smart person works outside a manager's jurisdiction"(Fryer, 2001, pp. 120-121).

Generally, Pragmatists tend to focus on the actions required to move a situation from the current or past reality toward a new desired outcome. They want to solve problems and bring plausible ideas into reality. They tend to seek a balanced inquiry through an exploration of multiple perspectives, as we will see in upcoming stories.

Originators—The Revolutionaries

Originators like to challenge current structure and systems. They encourage the exploration of new and alternative ideas and suggest possibilities that others have not imagined. Gary Hamel, author of *Leading the Revolution* and a strong advocate for change of the revolutionary type, says, "We live in a world where precedent has lost much of its imperial power. Rather than wasting energy in defending incrementalism against an imagined foe, corporate leaders should be working to build an innovative pipeline that is chock full of the kind of precedent-busting ideas that have the power to transform industries and to create new wealth. Oh, and on a final word to shareholders: Beware of the CEOs whose ambitions stretch no further than the incremental" (Hamel, 2001, p. 154).

Originators tend to focus on new possibilities, new vision and new direction. They encourage organizations to begin new tasks sooner rather than later. They often show a propensity for action but may not be effective implementers, as we will see in upcoming stories.

A Continuum of Preferences

The three Change Style Preferences fall along a linear continuum extending from Conservers at one extreme to Originators at the other, with Pragmatists in the middle. About 25 percent of the general population are Conservers and 25 percent are Originators. Half of the general population are Pragmatists. A quick way to describe each group's sensibilities is to compare them to farmers, hunters and explorers.

Change Style Preferences are real. They are a collection of beliefs, attitudes, behaviors and thought processes that describe how people accept, manage and instigate change. People encounter these Change Style Preferences in various degrees every day in their dealings with others and exhibit their own Change Style Preferences just as readily when faced with an opportunity for change.

Table 1: Change Style Preference Distributions

Conservers—25% of the General Population	Pragmatists—50% of the General Population	Originators—25% of the General Population
Conservers are similar to farmers, knowing they will harvest exactly what they plant. Conservers follow a prescribed routine and procedure for growing each crop, working by the seasons and following a predictable process. They learn from their own experience and that of others. They experiment only in small changes from the proven methods or on small trial plots. They cannot afford to risk the success of an entire season's crop by adopting an unproven method.	Pragmatists are similar to hunters. They know how to track, kill, dress and cure the meats of various animals. Pragmatists know the sight and range of the blowguns and bows, and the value of darts and arrows. They know when and where to find game, but do not always know in advance what game they will find in a day. They understand how their prey thinks and lives, adapting their own behaviors to find that prey. Hunters may set out to track one animal but are open to other possibilities. They seldom go hungry because their goal is to feed their families and the village. Hunters rely on proven tools and techniques. They prefer to stay within the bounds of their territorial hunting grounds. However, in difficult times they develop new techniques and move beyond the safety of familiar territory.	Originators are similar to explorers. Originators head into unknown lands and waters without the least notion of what they will find. They may go for the sake of going. They may adapt to the conditions they find, but prefer to change the conditions to their own liking. They are prepared for the unexpected but do not plan for every eventuality.

Conserver, Pragmatist and Originator Change Style Preferences

Now that we know the Conserver, Pragmatist and Originator characteristics, let's explore how they deal with change.

The Conserver[2] Preference

Conservers prefer to work within the existing structure and to create incremental changes. When facing change, Conservers:

- Generally appear deliberate, disciplined and organized.
- Prefer change that maintains the current structure.
- May operate from conventional assumptions.
- Enjoy predictability.
- May appear cautious and inflexible.
- Honor tradition and established practice.

Driving Us Crazy: The Conserver Viewpoint

You are headed home late at night on a familiar stretch of highway. Yours is the only car on the road. As you approach the intersection the light changes from green to yellow. You feel a momentary frustration because you know from experience that this light has a long cycle and seems to stay red forever. What do you do?

Conservers regard traffic lights as essential. Conservers appreciate the rules and value traffic lights for what they represent (i.e., a system for assuring safety and order). Conservers value the rules not so much for the sake of rules but for what rules represent. They know that without some rules to guide drivers, roads would be chaotic places. Traffic lights bring order to the roadways and ensure against chaos. As a consequence, Conservers would likely sit through a red light late at night with no other cars in sight and wait patiently until the light changes before proceeding.

More Detail on Conservers

- **Conservers generally prefer gradual and incremental change.** They are evolutionists rather than revolutionists. They want to see the existing structure retained with improvements. Conservers prefer to solve problems and to improve efficiency while maintaining the continuity and stability of current systems and structure.
- **Conservers prefer a secure work environment that is free from unexpected disruptions and surprise changes.** They prefer predictability and are attracted to stable, structured and orderly workplaces. Conservers like to be rewarded for contributing at a steady and consistent pace. They appreciate having the time and a place for reflection.
- **Conservers appear disciplined and organized.** They notice details and they act deliberately. They know the rules, the regulations and policies of the domains in

which they live and work. They prefer to live by those rules. For the Conserver, rules and regulations have inherent value. Without them, Conservers believe, the world would have no order and chaos would reign.

- **Conservers are skilled at attending to details and facts** in ways similar to those used by Sensors as defined by the Myers-Briggs Type Indicator.[3] For that reason, bankers, certain engineers, teachers, accountants and others whose professions require close attention to detail and structure tend to operate with a Conserver Change Style Preference. However, this attention to detail can obscure the Conserver's understanding of the "big picture." Conservers sometimes simply assume that everyone else sees what they see.

- **Conservers prefer tested and proven solutions.** In an evaluation of alternative approaches, Conservers look for proven examples of what has worked elsewhere. They want to see a track record with evidence of effective performance. Conservers embrace tradition and convention; they rely on the predictability that experience affords. Conservers do not "bet the bank" on unproven investments.

- **Conservers prefer to involve groups in making decisions and solving problems.** On the positive side, this approach includes more perspectives. On the negative side, it invites frequent and long committee meetings and bureaucratic barriers. At times, the Conserver's attention to the details of the process can actually impede the completion of the task, though they may not see that as a negative. A jury trial in a court of law is a good example of a Conserver-favored judicial system. It is slow and methodical with rules of evidence and clearly established procedures and precedents. Conservers are more likely than other Change Style Preferences to be aware of political turf and sensitivities that can aid or impede an organizational effort.

The Pragmatist Preference

Pragmatists deal in outcomes and seek practical, functional solutions to problems. When facing change, Pragmatists:

- May appear practical, agreeable and flexible.
- Operate as mediators and catalysts for understanding.
- Are open to both sides of an argument.
- May take more of a middle-of-the-road approach.
- Appear more team-oriented.

Driving Us Crazy: The Pragmatist Viewpoint

The Pragmatist respects the purpose of the traffic light, but also appreciates when it is appropriate and when it is not. Late at night, with no other cars in sight, a Pragmatist is likely to come to a full stop, look carefully for cross traffic and for a police car, then proceed. Pragmatists do not object to breaking the rules on moral grounds; they just want to ensure that the purpose of the rule has been served and that they do not get caught. For the Pragmatist, the "go, no go" decision may not be so much about the merits of the traffic light and laws as it is about the consequences of breaching the rules. The decision to stay or to go may hinge on the specifics of the situation (i.e., who is with them, recent violations, sobriety, etc.) and the degree of urgency they are facing. Pragmatists will consider the potential payoffs and weigh the costs.

More Detail on Pragmatists

- **Pragmatists are the peacemakers and the "middle-of-the-roaders."** They seek compromise to arrive at a solution that provides a workable outcome. If necessary, they will settle for a solution that is less than optimal rather than be stuck in a "no action" situation. To a Pragmatist, a less-than-optimal solution is better than no solution.

- **Pragmatists often appear reasonable and practical.** They listen to supporting arguments and look for practical results that accomplish the intended goals, often without regard to politics or egos.[4]

- **Pragmatists are usually agreeable and flexible.** They can see arguments from different perspectives and can value the contributions of others. Their flexibility can allow them to be pulled in many directions and can appear to be indecisiveness. In their willingness to seek a compromise position, Pragmatists sometimes appear to be noncommittal. Others may regard them as too quick to compromise.

- **Pragmatists like change that emphasizes practical and workable outcomes.** Pragmatists focus on the results and the effective functioning of the organizational system rather than on the organizational structure or politics. If adjusting the existing structure rather than re-engineering it presents a workable solution, Pragmatists will favor this solution because it is faster to implement. If the simple solution is not workable, they will readily accept making a more radical change.

- **Pragmatists appear to be more team-oriented** than do either Conservers or Originators.[5] They are interested in hearing all ideas and getting everyone's perceptions on the table for the group's consideration.

- **Pragmatists are less likely than Originators or Conservers to have hidden agendas.** They tend to have fewer "axes to grind" and fewer "points to prove" than those who are committed to maintaining the status quo or to challenging it.

- **Pragmatists are mediators.** Because they see the views of both Conservers and Originators, Pragmatists often serve as bridges of understanding between the two groups. The merit they are willing to place upon both perspectives can afford the Pragmatist a unique role in bridging between factions and in providing objective critique.

- **Pragmatists like an action-oriented workplace that engages others in a harmonious and participative atmosphere.** They prefer an environment that is flexible and adaptive, one that responds to current pressures. Pragmatists also like to be involved in hands-on experiences rather than theoretical discussions. They want adequate opportunities to discuss various options with coworkers. When harmony is not possible, then pragmatists may withdraw from the debate or settle for a less-than-optimal solution.

The Originator Preference

Sometimes Originators favor something that's different because it is just that—different. When facing change, Originators:

- May appear unorganized, undisciplined, unconventional and spontaneous.
- Prefer change that challenges current structure.
- Will likely challenge accepted assumptions.
- Enjoy risk and uncertainty.
- May be impractical and miss important details.
- May appear as visionary and systemic in their thinking.
- Can treat accepted policies and procedures with little regard.

Driving Us Crazy: The Originator Viewpoint

Originators see the traffic light as serving the specific purpose of controlling traffic so people do not get hurt. They respect the purpose, not the rule. From their perspective, the traffic light imposes limitations on their freedom to drive. These limitations are acceptable to them when danger is present. They believe they should not be penalized for moving through the red light if no cars are coming. "I can decide when it's safe to proceed," they say. Late at night with no other cars in sight, Originators may tap the brakes (just to make sure the coast is clear) and keep going. If they are sure no one will be injured (that is the purpose of the light after all), then the light itself has lost its value. Consequently, it becomes an encumbering structure limiting movement and wasting time.

More Detail on Originators

- **Originators prefer quick and expansive change.** They favor revolution over evolution. They approach life as an imperative to discard the old and to bring in the new as often and as quickly as possible. Originators will add to and build upon the ideas of others, taking their thinking in directions that others may not see as helpful or connected, even though the Originator's logic makes perfect sense to him/her.
- **Originators are often viewed in organizations as the change-agent.** They may be the ones who cause new things to happen and encourage goals to be accomplished in new ways.
- **Originators tend to loathe repetitive tasks.** Doing the same job in the same way with the expectation of getting the same result holds no charm for Originators. When a job does not require creativity or ingenuity, they may look for an alternate way to do the job. If they cannot find one, they may abandon the job.
- **Originators may appear undisciplined and unconventional.** They may seem to be making up rules as they go along and perhaps experimenting. Desks may be cluttered and work spaces chaotic, suggesting disorganization. However, an Originator can often reach into an overwhelming pile of papers and books and produce the very document

they were asked to retrieve. They may simply have a different "system" of organization.

- **Originators often challenge existing assumptions, rules and regulations.** Tradition and history are of less value to Originators than are future possibilities. They would tend to agree with Voltaire's statement, "Beaten paths are for beaten men."
- **Originators are often regarded as visionary, "out-of-the-box" thinkers.** They frequently attempt to solve problems in ways that challenge existing norms. They tend to favor the new and the different, the innovative and the adventurous. They like to try untested solutions, convinced by their own evaluations that these ideas will work.
- **Originators may appear impulsive.** They are often ready and eager to move ahead even though it appears that they have not closely considered the consequences of the proposed change. Originators may take new and unexpected directions.
- **Originators are risk-takers.** They are willing to take a calculated risk to test out new methods and approaches when they are convinced of the idea's value.
- **Originators are idea people.** They may favor ideas and concepts and the contributions of individuals more than they regard relationships and interpersonal processes. They would rather work alone than collaborate with others to "end up with" (as opposed to "create") something they would regard as a watered-down version of an original idea.

You Call the Shots

While a person may be closely described by the characteristics of a particular Change Style, one is not limited to only those behaviors, attitudes, values and beliefs. Change Styles are preferences. Similar to left-handedness or right-handedness, people have distinct and natural preferences, but also maintain the capacity to develop other skills through conscious effort.

To consciously choose to behave differently, you must first be aware of personal preference. With that knowledge, you can then practice behaving in concert with other Change Style Preferences when there is an advantage in doing so. Taking note of what works and what doesn't can help effective leaders become more comfortable with operating in ways that are different from their natural tendencies. These leaders know that no one Change Style Preference is better than another or more preferable from an organization's perspective. Indeed, each Change Style Preference adds value to the organization and to society when it is displayed effectively.

Notes

[1]   The Change Style Preferences presented in this book are measured by the Change Style Indicator (CSI) which has been used with over 150,000 people. The CSI norms reveal differences by profession, industry, gender and Myers-Briggs Type. Current CSI norms are available at the Discovery Learning Web site: www.discoverylearning.com. To obtain a copy of the CSI, contact Discovery Learning, Inc. at 336.272.9530 or via email at *info@discoverylearning.com*. CSI is available in a self-scored and on-line format.

[2]   The term Conserver connotes the sense of the word "conservation" consistent with historical or environmental conservation. It connotes preserving, retaining and protecting that which is of value. It should not be misconstrued as "conservative," especially in the political sense.

[3]   For a comparison of Change Style Indicator and Myers-Briggs Type Indicator comparative norms see the normative data section of the Discovery Learning, Inc. Web site (www.discoverylearning.com). All data at the site can be downloaded for no charge.

[4]   Research reveals that Pragmatists can readily identify their own Pragmatist characteristics while strong Conservers and Originators

are less effective at identifying the characteristics of their respective Change Style Preferences (Musselwhite, 2000).

5   Of the three Change Styles, Originators are perceived by their colleagues to be the least team-oriented and are perceived as more focused on individual contributions (Musselwhite, 2000).

Chapter 4

WORKING WITH OTHERS

Developing Awareness of
Change Style Perspectives and Perceptions

In This Chapter

As we saw in Chapter 3, people at work, at home, in their communities and in the world at large prefer to approach change differently. Some are Conservers, some are Pragmatists and some are Originators. But the fact is, regardless of personal preferences, people have to interact and cooperate for any organization or community to function successfully. This chapter explores two important steps in understanding how to effectively navigate change. These steps are:

- An awareness of the power of our personal *perspectives* and mind-sets, which form the basis of our Change Style Preference.
- An awareness of our *perceptions*, often negative, that are generated by our Change Style Preferences.

Additionally, we will show how these perspectives and perceptions play out in terms of how Conservers see Originators, how Originators see Conservers, and how Pragmatists are seen by both Conservers and Originators.

Perspective

Do you see what I see?

In the tale of the "Emperor's New Clothes," the people of the village, the members of the royal court and the king himself saw what they wanted to see (or what they thought they were supposed to see). Only when a boy of the village dared to tell what he really saw did all the others realize how they had been duped by two crafty con-artists posing as tailors with a special cloth they said "only wise people could see." The boy was unbridled by the position, expectations and ego that fashioned the perspectives of the others. Although his "truth," as shared from his perspective, was unwelcome and embarrassing, in the end it was valuable to everyone, including the king.

It is not uncommon in organizations for people to espouse views and convictions without seeing the limitations imposed by these perspectives. Perspectives are the product of how people process their knowledge and experience. Since no two people have the same set of experiences, no two people will have the same perspective. For this reason, it is useful—and some would say essential—to explore multiple perspectives when dealing with any complex issue. Our perspectives frame what we expect to see and our perceptions influence our interpretation of what we see. At the heart of both is our mind-set.

Mind-sets

Our mind-set is the way we see and interpret the world around us. It is the beliefs we hold and the assumptions we make without questioning. That basic human rights should not be violated for the benefit of the larger community is a western mind-set. In Iceland, babies are put out in strollers in the winter for an hour or so each day to make them healthier. This is also a mind-set. Sherpas, the indigenous mountain guides of the Himalayas, do not climb Mount Everest without first praying to Chomolungma, the Tibetan Mother Goddess of the mountain. For them, climbing the mountain is a sacred act and they will only be safe if Chomolungma is satisfied. In contrast, most western climbers see the mountain as a challenge to be won through their will, determination and expertise. These are contrasting mind-sets.

Cognitive scientists believe that human language primarily defines reality by shaping thought. Consequently, the meaning and interpretations that people attach to words and symbols form the basis of perceived reality. Understanding this concept is critical to effective communication. When a conclusion has been reached, persuasive arguments or even facts may not change a mind-set. The reality formed by the meaning one assigns to words and other symbols is more powerful than facts and persuasion.

The power of mind-set is supported by the experience of theorists and practitioners. Processes for appropriately questioning mind-set is the hallmark of effective coaching (in sports or business) and an essential ingredient of effective development, both personal and professional. Peter Senge describes mind-set as mental models, "deeply engrained assumptions, generalizations or even pictures or images that influence how we understand the world and how we take action. Very often we are not consciously aware of our mental models or the effects they have on our behavior" (Senge, 1990, p.18).

James Selman[1] views mind-set as "cognitive blindness"— not being aware of not knowing what one does not know. Selman uses the phrase "already listening" to describe pre-existing perspectives and beliefs about something. "Unless you are listening for something new, you cannot hear it." The corollary is that one will hear what one anticipates hearing.

Harvard psychologist Chris Argyris explains the defenses surrounding "already listening" and "mental models" in *Reasoning, Learning and Action: Individual and Organizational.* Argyris says that while people may not behave congruently with their stated or espoused beliefs, their behavior does typically reflect their "theories in use"—their "mental models." Argyris suggests that defensive routines develop to protect people from the discomfort of facing the gap between their espoused theories and their theories in action. He suggests these defensive routines become self-sealing, thus obscuring their own existence. This concept of mind-set is at the very heart of prejudice, whether based on socioeconomic, racial, ethnic, cultural, gender or personality differences.

Albert Einstein is credited with stating that common sense is nothing more than a set of prejudices put in place prior to the age of 18. He credited his childlike inquisitiveness as the reason for his probing questions about how the universe actually works. Others had ceased asking questions and had blindly accepted as "truth" what others said, proudly proclaiming: "Of course the sun revolves around the earth," "Man will never fly," "Send pictures and voice through the air? Impossible!"

The Full Picture

Certainly, the diverse characteristics of Conservers, Pragmatists and Originators provide rich opportunities for working together and for collaborating. Perhaps, more to the point, the absence of the perspective offered by any one of these Change Style Preferences could diminish the efforts of the group and leave gaping holes in a group's understanding of a particular issue. But, when embraced and appreciated, the various perspectives of Conservers, Pragmatists and Originators can create rich, though not always simple and easy, collaboration. The next section explores negative perceptions, the main obstacles to helpful collaboration.

Perceptions

Beauty is in the eye of the beholder.

If human perspectives are how one sees the world, then perceptions are the interpretation one attributes to what is seen. Being eyeball-to-eyeball is not the same as seeing eye-to-eye. Differences in perspective can lead to cooperation or conflict. How one perceives the actions and intentions of others is critical to how willing one is to work with them for a common purpose.

The more broadly people draw their circles of inclusiveness, the more diverse are the opinions, belief systems and rules for living that they confront. As the world grows smaller, we face the growing possibility that we will encounter and work with people who share very different perspectives—people with different cultural experiences and different mind-sets. For many people, perception follows the model that states, "Since I am right and I know that I am, and since you do not agree with me, then you must be wrong." Such blind allegiance to personal perception is the source of much continuing and costly personal and organizational warfare. Much of the conflict that arises in organizations today can be better understood and managed more effectively by addressing the perceptions that emerge as a result of different perceptions about change.

When you are aware of Change Style Preferences, you can reframe the conflict of "right" versus "wrong" to one of surfacing and exploring legitimate and valued differences. You can manage these differences by respecting the perceptions of others and create better outcomes than if you let any single perspective rule. Next, let's take a look at how the different Change Styles perceive each other.

Perceptions—Conservers Look at Originators

That's the craziest idea I've ever heard!

Comments from Conservers about Originators:

- He's divisive.
- She's impulsive.
- He lacks appreciation for tested ways of getting things done.
- She's always starting but not finishing projects.
- He is not interested in follow-through.
- She seems to want change for the sake of change.
- He just does not seem to understand how things get done.

When Originators suggest making rapid, wholesale changes to what Conservers might view as a "pretty good" system, Conservers see Originators as disloyal, disruptive and generally lacking appreciation for how things "really get done around here." Conservers see Originators as insensitive to the feelings of others, especially those who have built and nurtured the current structure. Conservers fear the disruption and turbulence that Originators can create in a workplace. They may even accuse Originators of wanting change just for the sake of making change, which for the Conserver is akin to stupidity. Conservers also believe that Originators are the people who like to start things, but who may not follow through with implementation.

"Hard Hats" and "Hippies"— Conservers vs. Originators

During the late 1960s, the anti-war protests on college campuses, the Summer of Love and the Woodstock Rock Festival were clearly the manifestations of Originators.[2] "Hippies" were trying to change the social system created by the World War II generation, which saw itself as having saved the world from would-be dictators, making it "safe for democracy." Conservers, stereotyped as politically conservative construction workers (the "Hard hats"), saw "Hippies" as impulsive, live-for-the-moment, lazy, social misfits who were oblivious to real threats and who had no appreciation for the sacrifices made by others to protect the system that secured them the freedoms they took for granted.

In organizations, the conflict between Originators and Conservers may not be so public. Organizational functions such as accounting (which have a relatively large number of Conservers) may feel threatened and devalued by functions such as sales and marketing. Sales and marketing (which often have a high percentage of Originators)[3] may consistently challenge organizational norms. In such cases, the tensions are often just below the surface.

Organizations that have operated in a consistent and stable business environment for years generally have a higher percentage of Conservers than companies in general. When such organizations change and Originators are recruited (typically, very few have been nurtured by the existing organization), they can be seen as outside agitators and troublemakers. The opinion of Conservers is often, "They are not 'one of us' and cannot be trusted." Or, "They are just plain wacky."

This happened in the electric utility industry in the early and mid-'90s. This had been a highly regulated industry since its inception, with no competition. If operating costs increased then the company petitioned its state utility board for a rate increase. When deregulation began in the early '90s, executives were stunned. When competitors appeared at their back door, their first response was to call their attorneys—a very structural approach to dealing with the problem. Many of these companies found themselves without the innovative thinkers to lead them through this changing market. Employees who were not comfortable with the predictability and structure of the electric utility industry had long since moved on to other industries. Those who remained were generally marginalized because they did not reflect the predominant culture of the industry.

Perceptions—Originators Look at Conservers

Get your head out of the sand.
Comments from Originators about Conservers:

- He is dogmatic.
- She is such a bureaucrat.
- He always yields to authority.
- She prefers the status quo.
- He seems to be lacking in new ideas.
- She is so political.
- He has his head in the sand.

Originators can see Conservers as locked blindly in bureaucratic, dogmatic thinking. They see Conservers as too willing to "go along to get along" without testing the validity of their assumptions. Originators see Conservers as the keepers of the status quo with no new ideas of their own.

Conservers might look at a given system and the proven results and say, "Not bad. Maybe we can trim a little here and add a little there, but all in all, not bad." Originators might look at the same situation and while theorizing about potential goals conclude, "We can't get there from here. We'll have to go somewhere else to start. Follow me." Originators would see the Conservers' preference for sticking with the current system as a limiting factor in getting the organization where it needs to be.

"Question Authority"—Another View of Conservers vs. Originators

One of the battle cries of the social revolutionaries in the '60s was "Question Authority," an admonition born of an original mind. It directly confronted the cultural thinking of a generation that came of age under the leadership of a more authoritarian, top-down leadership mind-set. Either people had fought in World War II and had survived by following orders or they had worked as part of an assembly line in the defense plants, producing munitions, planes, ships and tanks. Together they had sacrificed and rationed for the "greater good." The idea of questioning an order was counter to being "a good soldier." In the extreme and in the mind of some Conservers, such questioning was tantamount to treason. The Originators, often lacking an appreciation for that personal history and wanting to challenge authority, launched into a mode of "that was then, this is now." They saw the Conservers as stuck in time and operating under old assumptions that no longer applied as commerce blossomed in international markets and the United States began trading with those whom it previously had fought. Originators see a new world with new opportunities. They see Conservers as getting in the way.

In companies where knowledge is critical, such as the software and high-tech industries, new ideas are the currency of success. Loyalty, hard work and seniority have less value to Originators who are looking to gain the next competitive edge through a leap in capability fostered by the next and newest "great idea." Such industries attract Originators. Although persons in these organizations charged with running operational functions (often detail-oriented Conservers) are making substantial contributions to the organization, they may feel that their contributions are not valued as much as those of Originators.

Perceptions—Pragmatists as Seen by Both Conservers and Originators

Just get off the fence.

Comments about Pragmatists from strong Conservers and Originators:

- She shifts with the changing wind.
- He is so compromising.
- She is so indecisive.
- He is so easily influenced.
- She can never commit.
- He hides behind his team's needs.

Although Conservers and Originators can readily identify each other as those with whom they may disagree and are frequently at odds, Pragmatists may find they are sometimes at odds with both of these types. A strength of the Pragmatist is the ability to see the perspectives of others including avowed Conservers and strong Originators. However, both of these groups (at their relative extremes) may see Pragmatists as noncommittal, indecisive, wishy-washy and even "spineless." They may see Pragmatists as flip-flopping from one position to another when, in fact, the Pragmatists may sincerely appreciate and understand both Conserver and Originator perspectives.

Conversely, and more often the case, Pragmatists are viewed by both Conservers and Originators as potential allies in advancing and helping others understand their positions. Pragmatists may find themselves heavily recruited by factions on both ends of the Change Style continuum to help build support for their positions and coalitions for their ideas.

Because Pragmatists operate in a middle ground on the Change Style continuum, sometimes they are seen differently by strong Conservers and strong Originators. Conservers may see Pragmatists as too flexible. Originators may see them as too sentimental or considerate. But Pragmatists form their own opinions as well and may see both Conservers and Originators as inflexible, entrenched, and rigidly and selfishly committed to singular views.

The fact is, Pragmatists are more interested in getting to a workable solution that serves an existing need than in endlessly debating the philosophies of dissimilar groups. So although they may appreciate and understand the views of Conservers and Originators, Pragmatists may get frustrated with what appears to be the pushing of ideological positions at the expense of taking effective action. Pragmatists are motivated to act and then move on. Unfortunately, this eagerness for action can lead Pragmatists to settle for less-than-optimal solutions. To that end, Pragmatists should check their planned actions against their intentions.

One of the insights attendant to learning one's Change Style Preference is that this developed preference may, in fact, be directing one's perspective of events and interactions and be coloring one's perceptions of others in ways that are unknown to the individual. The challenge for every person—Conserver, Pragmatist or Originator—is to raise his/her level of thinking about interactions to a new plane and to question his/her perspective and perceptions. If one can do this effectively, one can see opportunities for overcoming limited thinking, hear what others are actually saying and expand the collective potential of the group or the organization.

Notes

[1] James Selman, seminar notes from the Canadian Centre for Management Development, Ottawa, January 2000.

[2] Analysis of the Change Style Indicator database reveals interesting generational differences. People who came of age during the 1940s and 1990s have very similar Change Style profiles: 25 percent Conservers, 50 percent Pragmatists, and 25 percent Originators. People who came of age in the 1960s and early 1970s have a strikingly different distribution with 37 percent Originators. This raises the question: Were they influenced by the social revolution of the '60s or did the revolution occur because of a generation with a disproportionate number of Originators?

[3] From the Change Style Indicator database, accountants are 27 percent Conservers, 58 percent Pragmatists and 15 percent Originators. By contrast, people who identify marketing and sales as their profession have strikingly different profiles. Marketing is 10 percent Conservers, 46 percent Pragmatists and 44 percent Originators, while sales is 10 percent Conservers, 54 percent Pragmatists and 36 percent Originators.

Part Two

O nce you can differentiate between an individual's Change Style Preference and an individual's competence at managing change, you can begin to appreciate and benefit from contributions each makes to the organization's effectiveness and productivity. Knowing the limitations of each style, including your own, is crucial in understanding Change Style Preference and recognizing opportunities for effective and efficient use of Change Styles.

For Better or Worse

Each of the three Change Styles can be used effectively or ineffectively; the outcomes can be strikingly different. An effective Conserver will contribute differently to the group's work process than will an ineffective Conserver. This is also true for Pragmatists or Originators. All three Change Styles are part of the full fabric of change and are of equal value to an organization when they are carried out effectively. However, when these same Change Styles are emphasized too much at the wrong time in a change process or carried out ineffectively, they can create conflicts and problems for individuals, for work teams and for the entire organization.

Knowing the difference between effective and ineffective behavior is sometimes more difficult than one might think, especially for persons who operate from a Change Style Preference different from that being observed. For example, to the extreme Conserver, all behavior of Originators may look disruptive when, in fact, some actions may be exactly what the situation calls for. To avoid confusing competence with style, it is important not only to understand the styles but to be capable of distinguishing between effective and ineffective manifestations of each style.

In this section we will show the qualities and behaviors associated with each Change Style. Six stories present how the Change Style Preferences of Conservers, Pragmatists and Originators contribute to and detract from positive outcomes when they are performed effectively and ineffectively. These stories are based on real situations. Names and identifying information have been changed to protect the privacy and anonymity of the organizations and the individuals involved.

Chapter 5

THE CONSERVERS

What Works, What Doesn't

In This Chapter

In this chapter we will explore effective and ineffective Conserver behaviors. A case study will illustrate both sides of this Change Style. We will also explore:

- Contributions to the organization.
- Leadership style.
- Potential pitfalls.
- Prescriptive remedies.

Effective Conserver Behavior

The effective Conservers in an organization understand how all the parts are connected. They grasp the system of which they are a part and recognize the need to improve it with continual, focused efforts. They know the details and the history of the organization. Effective Conservers know who is invested strongly in what arenas and whose buy-in is essential to implement any changes. They are in tune with the culture of their organizations. They respect the rules, but they are willing to change the rules by working through the system.

Effective Conserver behavior is reflected in the work of land and nature conservancies and the historic preservationists who organize, raise money and purchase properties they want to save rather than waiting for government to act. Effective Conservers understand the value of having their thinking challenged because they know they sometimes miss new opportunities and possibilities. They are the diligent researchers who stick to a planned regimen. Effective Conservers know how the system operates and who can provide good information. They know how to get things done without creating unnecessary reaction and opposition.

The following story illustrates an effective Conserver. It tells how one business professional used her awareness of her own limitations and the spirit of team building to create a system for continual improvement in her division's performance.

Case Study: Banking on Getting Better

"I can plot the course and set the sails, but it really helps to have others up in the crow's nest scanning the horizon."

Nancy was good at the operational details that had made her regional bank one of the most efficient financial institutions in the nation. Her success helped make her an executive vice president. She had good systems in place as well as the technology to run them efficiently. She refined and updated the systems regularly. The bottom-line results she produced were evidence of her capability.

Still, she was aware that the financial industry was changing. Mergers were changing the competitive landscape and the ways banks did business. She knew that what had helped her bank be successful yesterday might not be adequate tomorrow.

She wanted a process in place for evaluating opportunities and exploring new business areas. She knew it would work if she could make it a standard process.

Knowing that her strength was in effectively managing existing systems, she established a team of subordinate colleagues and challenged them to think "out of the box" about new business opportunities and new technologies. It was her "vision and idea" team. They met with her monthly for two hours and presented new ideas they had just encountered or had considered already and perhaps believed were worthy of further investigation. This team was encouraged to plan the best use of this two-hour meeting so that their priorities for presenting ideas did not get lost to the overzealous interests of one or two people. It was a time to get away from the current reality of how they did what they did and to think about creating new ways to serve existing and potential clients with innovative and different services. Sometimes the team concentrated on refining ideas already introduced. Other times, it focused on solving existing problems. They also used the sessions to explore and create criteria for evaluating ideas with both long-term and short-term horizons.

She knew her strengths and knew where she most needed help from others. She created a system that institutionalized the process of innovative thinking and of looking at emerging issues that challenged existing operations and systems. As a result, her bank led the industry in the implementation of innovations. This happened because the whole system supported innovation and new initiatives. When it came time to introduce an alternative approach, the ideas had already been considered, challenged and questioned from every angle. No stone had been left unturned. Implementation went smoothly because everyone involved had commitment. Today, Nancy's bank is considered one of the most competitive regional banks in the United States.

Effective Conservers respect the existing structure and work with the input of knowledgeable participants to improve performance bit by bit over time. They understand the value of having their thinking challenged.

Qualities of Effective Conservers

Although a specific person may not exhibit all of the following traits, they help describe in general the observable behaviors of an effective Conserver. When leading a change effort, an effective Conserver may:

- See the details of a situation.
- Understand the mechanics of how the organization works.
- Respect rules and regulations, but can work to change them.
- Be cognizant of the culture of the organization.
- Be aware of relationships within the organization.
- Know the vested interest of particular persons in the organization.
- Anticipate how particular individuals will respond to proposed changes.
- Identify problems in the system's mechanics.
- Know who can provide good information.
- Know how to integrate and coordinate efforts.
- Know how to work through existing systems and structure for change.
- Generate trust and confidence in the organization about change.
- Ask open and positive questions about changes and the need for change.

Contributions to the Organization

Conservers contribute to the organization by:

- Working to get things done on schedule.
- Finding ways to continuously improve current processes and operating systems.
- Dealing with details and factual information.

- Working well within the existing organizational structure.
- Honoring commitments and playing by the rules.
- Following protocol and established traditions of getting things done.
- Encouraging others to follow the proven routine.
- Encouraging others to follow through on commitments to complete tasks as promised.
- Pushing for careful investigation of the consequences of change.
- Questioning the necessity and/or the scope of change.
- Handling day-to-day matters of their operations and tasks efficiently.

Leadership Style

As leaders, Conservers:

- Are steady, consistent, reliable.
- Expect the organizational policies, procedures and rules to be followed and reward those who do so.
- Facilitate the coordination and integration of ideas into the existing system.
- Promote continuous improvement.
- Encourage the traditional values of the organization while attending to its practical needs.

Ineffective Conserver Behavior

Knowing the price of everything and the value of nothing describes the ineffective Conserver. When performed ineffectively, the Conserver Change Style Preference focuses on the details while forgetting the overall objective for a project. Ineffective Conservers are the highway design engineers who continued for years building interstate highway signage stronger and more collision-resistant to reduce replacement costs before someone suggested using a breakaway design to save the lives of drivers. Consider Major-General Edward Braddock, a British army officer during the French and Indian War. He insisted on fighting in the standard regimental formation that had dominated the battlefields of Europe even though the Native American allies of the French were fighting "Indian-style" from behind trees and rocks. Braddock was killed and the British were routed by ambush near Fort Duquesne in 1755.

By focusing exclusively on the approved process and on the existing rules without regard to the changing circumstances or the purposes of an undertaking, Conservers become ineffective. They are also ineffective when they cannot recognize the input and perspective of others. That condition makes them a liability in a team effort because they can become stubbornly resistant to different or innovative ways of doing things.

The following story illustrates an ineffective Conserver. He is operating out of learned behavior without regard for the overall purpose of the rules being followed.

Case Study: Marching Orders

"We do things by the book around here, mister. We've got rules and we follow them. Everybody. All the rules, all the people, all the time. Do you understand me, soldier? Dismissed."

The target of this directive was a student, not a soldier, but he was enrolled at a military boarding school where discipline was strategic to achieving educational objectives. Sufficient structure and discipline were missing in the lives of many of the students. By providing it, the school was making excellent students of these young people. The rules were a means to an end. They provided order and a framework within which the educational process could take place among students who could too easily get distracted if they had the freedom to make all their own choices.

The school's new commandant was a retired Marine, a

decorated soldier. For him the expression "old habits die hard" was absolutely true. He knew how the Marine Corps operated and he had followed its regimen without deviation in a successful military career. Now he was looking to use this military training to help develop young people into productive citizens through the discipline of a regimented educational environment.

Unfortunately, the commandant sometimes became too focused on the rules and forgot the purpose for which they existed. He had been known to discipline a student for not polishing his uniform buttons or keeping his shoes polished to parade-dress standards even though the student was making excellent grades and was excelling in sports. The student was maturing and was developing self-esteem; but, as adolescents are prone to do, was also finding ways to rebel against the surrounding structure of the school. Instead of celebrating the student's achievements that, in part, were fostered by the discipline of the military regimen, the commandant tended to focus his attention on the strict observance of all rules. He forgot that students were not training for war, but were learning to set goals and to focus their energies on worthwhile accomplishments.

The commandant failed to see that, in this school setting, rules had a different purpose and had a different importance than in the Marines. The rules were intended as a means to an end, not as an end in themselves. To him, each and every rule had to be followed to the letter, even if doing so jeopardized achievement of the larger goal.

Ineffective Conservers often miss seeing the big picture and operate by the rules without regard to the objective for which the rules were created.

Qualities of Ineffective Conservers

Although a specific person may not exhibit all these traits, they help describe in general the observable behaviors that can affect a group's efforts to produce collectively when led by an ineffective Conserver. When leading a change effort, an ineffective Conserver may:

- Be bound by the rules, not the intentions behind them.
- Follow the rules regardless of the outcomes.
- Not see the big picture and focus only on pieces.
- Look at how change affects him or her without reference to the impact on the organization.
- Offer resistance in a negative way and alarm others.
- Catch people in lose-lose binds and give them no options.
- Appear to have a personal, self-serving agenda.
- Refuse to consider any ideas that have not been tested and proven effective elsewhere.

Potential Pitfalls for Conservers

Each of the Change Styles is subject to potential problems and pitfalls that can lead to ineffective behaviors. Conservers should be aware of their vulnerability to the following pitfalls:

- Conservers may become too rigid in thought and action.
- Conservers may be too set in their ways and appear stubborn or resistant.
- Conservers may stifle creativity and innovation in others by promoting too strongly the existing rules and policies.
- Conservers may delay action too long by reflecting unduly on a situation.
- Conservers may delay completion of tasks as well by focusing too strongly on perfection.
- Conservers may focus on small details and inconsistencies and fail to see beyond the immediate situation to understand the broader, strategic context.
- Conservers may criticize new ideas before investigating the advantages.

Prescriptive Remedies

To help avoid style preference traps and to increase their flexibility when anticipating or participating in a change effort, Conservers should consider the following strategies:

- Explore alternatives (perhaps a set number, such as a minimum of three) before making a decision.
- Do not announce a decision until considering at least one or two other possibilities.
- Explore the consequences of proposed actions, asking others for input if necessary.
- Ask a trusted Originator to share his or her perspective to gain insight and information.
- Ask someone to play the devil's advocate with the proposed solution.
- Write a list of imagined advantages from an Originator's perspective.
- Avoid relying on committees for problem solving and decision making unless absolutely necessary. When unavoidable, create three or four criteria against which decisions can be referenced by the committee.

Chapter 6

THE PRAGMATISTS

What Works, What Doesn't

In This Chapter

In this chapter we will explore effective and ineffective Pragmatist behaviors. A case study will illustrate both sides of this Change Style. We will also explore:

- Contributions to the organization.
- Leadership style.
- Potential pitfalls.
- Prescriptive remedies.

Effective Pragmatist Behavior

Getting things done is the hallmark of effective Pragmatists. They may not wait until they know what the exact, final outcome will be, but they initiate movement and get others involved.

They seek out and understand the range of viewpoints that others hold. Effective Pragmatists want to break deadlocks and encourage solutions that create forward movement. Movement towards a viable outcome is more important to the Pragmatist than are idealistic positions. They relate to the Originators who want to do something new and different right away. They can also relate to the Conservers who are concerned about the consequences of changing an existing system. Toward the "end game" of finding a workable outcome, effective Pragmatists identify the potential conflicts and manage the sharing of ideas and information that will help people see each other's positions.

In the wake of devastating violations of human rights committed during South Africa's apartheid, Archbishop Desmond Tutu oversaw an effort in national reconciliation by conducting hearings to reveal all that had happened. The purpose of the South African Truth and Reconciliation Commission was not to blame or to punish but rather to get all the facts and beliefs into a public forum and to allow people the opportunity to grieve, to repent and to forgive. Tutu knew that an effective and just democracy could not move forward in South Africa until people who had been hurt by past injustices could be heard. His goal was not to punish, to blame or to defend, but to minimize the impact of the past on the capacity of the new South Africa to move forward in a manner that could address the real needs of its many citizens.

The following story illustrates an effective Pragmatist. She is working to bring about change by engaging the efforts of people with very opposing and even antagonistic views.

Case Study: Making History

"Tourism as a business isn't just about filling up hotels. That 'heads-in-beds' approach is for the convention trade. Tourism is also about creating new experiences in different places."

The tourism industry in this southern state was steady. For several years, tourism promotion by the responsible state agency had subsisted under a caretaker philosophy.

The effort was constrained by a limited budget and frequent turnover of staff. The state's promotional efforts each year consisted of doing again what seemed to have worked reasonably well the year before. As a result, visitations were about the same each year and the revenue from tourism was flat.

Wanting to address the problem of flat growth, the executive director of the state's tourism division organized a gathering of longtime industry participants and interested people to get some ideas on what she could do to improve the performance of the division. People were generally glad to have been asked their opinions and many ideas were generated. The one that seized the attention of the group, however, was a presentation about the growth potential in promoting "heritage" tourism. The presenter, now a consultant, had been a tourism director in another state. He had arrived on the scene with interest and energy for introducing this idea for promoting heritage tourism in this state where he now lived.

The executive director liked the idea, too. She set out to help sell it to others. Knowing that the presenter was an outsider, the executive director suggested he move cautiously at first. She funded a small project to promote one particular aspect of the state's heritage. This approach gave her a track record and allowed her to introduce the concept as an opportunity that paralleled, augmented and added to what was perceived as already working well. For a while, the executive director followed the reactions and responses to the idea of heritage tourism. She listened and learned. She also helped the heritage tourism promoter become a colleague of those with vested interests in the way the industry operated.

Simultaneous with her efforts to win interest in the idea with the established industry, the executive director explored new partnerships with others, including state agencies that had not previously been involved in tourism promotion. She talked with museums, national parks, historic sites and others about coordinating new promotional efforts around various heritage themes. She met many other people who had innovative ideas about what the future could be for tourism in the state. She organized conferences to explore ideas about ways to draw tourists to the state. She listened and learned. The innovators felt included and welcomed; the established industry pushed for timetables for action and for declarations of budgets.

Eventually, her ability to marry new ideas with the existing industry attracted the attention of the state's legislature. She was able to lobby for a larger promotional budget and to implement many of the ideas that others had suggested. A new stability was achieved in the state's tourism industry. The tried-and-true ways of promoting tourism were enhanced by the infusion of new ideas.

As a result of this executive director's leadership efforts, the state gained a broader reputation for what it offered visitors. More tourists arrived each year spending more money in longer stays. Along with them came delegates from other states wanting to learn about this unique tourism promotion process that seemed to be working so well.

Effective Pragmatists bring together different perspectives and sometimes widely divergent agendas to help create outcomes that are satisfactory to all.

Qualities of Effective Pragmatists

Although a specific person may not exhibit all of the following, they help describe in general the observable behaviors of an effective Pragmatist. When leading a change effort, an effective Pragmatist may:

- Work for practical results.
- Keep an open mind and be willing to explore different solutions.

- Respect different perspectives.
- Not appear to have a personal agenda.
- Focus on workable outcomes and not on ownership of the solution.
- Build team identity and cohesion while working with real issues.
- Move a group toward decision and action.

Contributions to the Organization

Pragmatists contribute to the organization by:

- Encouraging cooperation and compromise to get things done.
- Taking a realistic and practical approach, and tending to achieve goals in spite of the rules, rather than because of them.
- Being willing to address the problems of the organization as they arise.
- Drawing people together around a common purpose and helping them organize ideas into an action plan with specific outcomes.
- Appreciating what both the Conservers and the Originators can see and, as a result, being in a position to mediate the two views.
- Promoting practical organizational structures that deliver on the purpose of the organization.

Leadership Style

As leaders, Pragmatists:

- Are facilitators and mediators who lead by helping others solve their problems.
- Build cooperation rather than just expecting it.
- Adapt their experience to solve current problems.

- Encourage the organization to "walk the talk" and to achieve a congruence between values and actions.
- Push for open dialogue, encourage everyone's input and then push for closure and action.

Ineffective Pragmatist Behavior

Pragmatists are ineffective in an organization when they are frozen in uncertainty or indecision. Ineffective Pragmatists listen to everyone's point of view, but cannot choose a course of action that favors one position over another. They sympathize with everyone's perspective and then settle for middle-of-the-road compromises that smack of political expediency.

Ineffective Pragmatists often create additional problems for themselves and others by not taking timely action. They may become so concerned with pleasing everyone that no action is taken or the action that is taken is so compromised as to be ineffective.

The following story illustrates an ineffective Pragmatist. It shares the experience of a manager caught between two reasonable approaches to solving a problem, but whose indecision creates a situation with a less satisfactory outcome.

Case Study: The Art of Indecision

"I think you're both right, so let me think about it and I'll get back to you on that . . . sometime."

The consulting firm had relied on its in-house art department for years. This resource allowed them to provide their clients customized print materials on a timely basis. The firm had hundreds of clients and most of the workload arrived in three separate waves each year. At those times the small art department staff was swamped with work and the stress levels were high for everyone involved, especially the consultants working from several remote offices in other states who had promised that work would be delivered by certain dates.

The art department was operating in a fully digital mode and had all the capabilities that were needed for them to prepare files electronically for delivery to the commercial printer who would complete the task of printing the promised materials. However, what most encumbered the production process was securing the review and approval of consultants and clients. Currently, paper copies of the various print pieces were mailed to the consultants for review. This approval process took two or three weeks with multiple mailings and expensive overnight packages consuming precious time and potential project profits.

To help speed the review and approval process and to reduce the costs, the art director was pressing the division manager to purchase a high-end software package and color-corrected monitors that would enable the e-mailing of review copies to the remote consultants. This capability would allow the consultants to annotate and approve the various print pieces in less time than was now required. The art director expected it would not be long before such technology would dominate the graphic arts world, and he did not want to be left behind.

The division manager agreed that increasing productivity by shortening the review and approval process and minimizing costs was desirable for both the art department and the firm. He understood the potential payoff and saw the advantages that the art director had outlined. He confirmed this understanding in the most recent division meeting; his support was well received by the staff.

But now the division manager had just returned from a budget meeting with the company president where he was told that the last quarter of the year would be very tight. He was instructed to hold the line on expenses and all capital investments with less than a three-year life. He understood what the president was saying and agreed. He promised that he would do his part. This was certainly not the year to fall short on making one's numbers. The company needed good financials for a planned merger, and the manager needed the annual bonus to pay for a remodeled nursery at home. A baby was on the way.

The manager agreed with the arguments that both the president and the art director were making. They were both logical and well reasoned. If he bought the software system and color-corrected monitors that required installation at the several remote sites, he would win the enthusiastic support of the art department staff and give them the tools they wanted and needed, but he would do so at the risk of missing his numbers. If he did not buy the system, he might make his numbers this quarter, but he could jeopardize productivity in the art department. Keeping his boss happy certainly seemed a wise and worthwhile objective, but then again, he knew that he had to see and work with the art department staff every day. Making either side unhappy would be a problem.

At the next staff meeting, the art director shared that he had just learned something that sweetened the deal. If the purchase of the software and monitors were made in the next two weeks, the vendor could offer a 25 percent discount and still provide the training. A newer and more expensive version of the color-corrected monitors had just been announced and the vendor wanted to clear his inventory. He only had six units left and he wanted to know if the manager could buy them before next Wednesday.

On Wednesday afternoon, the manager got called into a meeting. Consequently, he was not available when the vendor called to say that he had another party interested in the monitors and needed a decision within the hour. In the end, neither the purchase nor the lease was made. An exasperated and frustrated art director left the company and went to work for a competitor. Some important projects were not completed by promised dates and a few key clients took their projects and their business elsewhere. The manager and the company both missed their financial numbers. The merger was consummated on unfavorable terms. The manager received no bonus.

Ineffective Pragmatists sympathize with opposing views and

see the logic and reasoning behind everyone's position, but they cannot take decisive action when needed.

Qualities of Ineffective Pragmatists

Although a specific person may not exhibit all of these traits, they help describe in general the observable behaviors that can affect a group's efforts to produce collectively when led by an ineffective Pragmatist. When leading a change effort, an ineffective Pragmatist may:

- Appear wishy-washy and indecisive.
- Be unable to make firm decisions.
- Play to the politics in a situation before committing.
- Propose benign, middle-of-the-road, problematic solutions when action is required.
- Operate with a self-serving personal agenda.
- Want to know where everyone stands on an issue before committing.

Potential Pitfalls for Pragmatists

Each of the Change Styles is subject to potential problems and pitfalls that can lead to ineffective behaviors. Pragmatists should be aware of their vulnerability to the following pitfalls.

- Pragmatists may appear to be noncommittal.
- Pragmatists may be indecisive and undirected.
- Pragmatists may try to please too many people at the same time.
- Pragmatists may compromise too readily to a "middle-of-the-road" position.
- Pragmatists may not promote their views strongly enough.
- Pragmatists may be too easily influenced.
- Pragmatists may wait too long to decide upon a course of action and fail as a consequence.

Prescriptive Remedies

To avoid style preference traps and to increase their flexibility when anticipating or participating in a change effort, Pragmatists should consider the following strategies:

- Identify specific questions to ask Originators and Conservers to broaden perspectives.
- Seek out people who are known to have strong preferences for Originator and Conserver styles to get input.
- Ask those with strong styles to respond from an emotional perspective. Ask questions such as "How do you feel about this?" and "How would you like things to be?"
- Imagine the consequences of a decision in the future at specific intervals, such as one year, five years and ten years if those are appropriate to the problem's nature.
- Imagine the effect of a proposed decision on someone for whom they care.
- Identify three or four high-priority criteria and then apply them to all the proposed solutions.
- Make a list of the perceived strengths and weaknesses for each potential course of action.

Chapter 7

THE ORIGINATORS

What Works, What Doesn't

In This Chapter

I n this chapter we will explore effective and ineffective
Originator behaviors. A case study will illustrate both sides
of this Change Style. We will also explore:

- Contributions to the organization.
- Leadership style.
- Potential pitfalls.
- Prescriptive remedies.

Effective Originator Behavior

Effective Originators may be the inventors of "the better
mousetraps" and many of the labor-saving devices of modern
civilization. Some are also the leaders of nations and promoters

of just causes in uncertain times. They see a need and a purpose, and they have a vision of the future. They know how to involve others who can manage the details and who can help make things happen. They may be the likes of Thomas Jefferson, Harriet Tubman, Henry Ford, Franklin D. Roosevelt and Mother Teresa, who dreamed of a different world and then worked cooperatively with others to bring their visions into reality.

Effective Originators are often the first to suggest an idea and to offer it for others to consider. But despite the celebrity enjoyed by the Originators mentioned above, many Originators are simply good at what they do; they become unsung heroes of the communities where they live and work. The following story shows how one such person with a vision for a better world worked to bring his idea into being.

Case Study: Growing Concerns

"Man does not live by bread alone. There'd better be a farmer out there somewhere with soil and water sufficient to cultivate the wheat."

That was the fervent belief out of which grew a statewide agricultural stewardship association. Those with an interest in the state's agricultural industry ranged from the large farmers and commercial growers who produced the bulk of this large agricultural state's salable products to the small organic growers who were interested in practicing environmentally sound agriculture and wanting others to do so as well. Included were the state's farm bureau, the state department of agriculture and the university extension service. Not surprisingly, these large bureaucracies had entrenched positions of power in the industry.

In the view of the environmentalists, the growers were using pesticides and fertilizers that were polluting both surface waters and ground waters as well as poisoning wildlife. To express their views, the environmentalists and organic farmers launched organized campaigns to publicly criticize the large growers.

They also lodged complaints to elected officials and levied charges to regulatory agencies. The growers resented these "attacks" by groups they considered both "fringe," and "radical" with no political clout. The two factions and those organizations caught in between were clearly at odds with one another. The atmosphere was one of enmity, not cooperation.

Into this fray stepped Jack with a vision for creating a better way for all groups involved to cooperate in support of something they all wanted: sustainable agriculture, whether defined in environmental or economic terms. He had a notion that society had better pay attention to how it produces the food that everyone needs without destroying the environment that supports all life. He also wanted at the same time to support the rural communities where the food is produced. With financial support from a large foundation and his own determination, patience and effective relationship-building skills, he set out to make this vision a reality.

While his heart was with the community of farmers that advocated an organic approach, he knew their voice would continue to be quite limited without economic, political and scientific support. Despite having no official standing in the industry other than the backing of the foundation, he intended to garner support for creating an umbrella organization that would recognize, champion and support the values of "sustainable" agriculture. His vision for this organization did not include how the organization would be structured, how it would operate or the projects it might undertake. His vision was focused on what the organization could accomplish. His primary argument was that, in some way, these various interests shared a focus on the broad issues of sustainable agriculture, whether this was translated as economic, environmental or philosophical. He approached each special interest group and told them of his vision. Then he listened openly and carefully to their ideas and their concerns. He created relationships with them one by one and gained their trust. He encouraged the participation of environmentalists, large commercial growers and family farmers. His knowledge of the scientific, economic and environmental issues won a degree of trust from the skeptics on each side. His arguments played to the rational interests of those he sought out rather than to their emotions. He won the support of the leadership of the Farm Bureau and the university's agricultural extension service by helping reduce the friction between the different industry factions.

He eventually invited representatives from the different organizations to attend a gathering. He hired a facilitator to lead these meetings in which participants used innovative processes to create pictures (actual drawings) of their individual visions for their communities. With these separate views, they worked collaboratively in mixed groups to build three-dimensional models of their integrated visions.

From their interaction, the parties began to create an organization that would share information among the different groups. Even if each party was not won over entirely, he had removed as a threat the belief that this growing movement for "responsible" agriculture was a threat. Within a year, a statewide association was formed that spanned all the agricultural organizations in the state. Since this group's inception, these organizations have been working together to inform decision-makers, to affect public policy and to support producers.

He did not seek a leadership role in the new association and shifted his attention to new efforts in the arena of sustainable agriculture. He continued to be a dues-paying member. He was able to keep his vision alive because he was open to others' ideas on the form this organization should take. Rather than push the specifics of his own vision, he brought together key stakeholders and let them participate early in the creation of a common vision. He was committed to not allowing any one group to dominate or alienate others. He was also willing to step aside and let the willing stakeholders assume the leadership as well as the management of details. Out of this effort emerged the state's Agricultural Stewardship Association that is today an influential force in the state and the nation. It includes many of the mainstream agricultural organizations whose participation is critical to the realization of his vision. He had a vision for a different way of doing things, and he was effective in how he brought his vision into reality.

Effective Originators maintain their original vision and can persuade others to join in without compromising what they set out to do. They understand the need to listen and to collaborate early in their efforts with effective implementers. They do not abandon their ideas and efforts before they have taken root. They also understand the need for building relationships.

Qualities of Effective Originators

Although a specific person may not exhibit all of the following traits, they help describe in general the observable behaviors of an effective Originator. When leading a change effort, an effective Originator will:

- Think into the future and see possibilities that others do not.
- Focus on the desired outcomes rather than change for the sake of change.
- Know how to engage others in discussions about change.
- Value and know how to use Conservers and Pragmatists for implementation.
- Challenge assumptions and conventions without challenging or attacking individuals.
- Get things started by taking the first steps.
- Take risks but have a contingency plan.
- Balance tasks and relationship issues.
- Know there may be multiple paths to the same destination.

Contributions to the Organization

Originators contribute to the organization by:

- Looking at the "big picture" and tending to approach problems by examining the system as a whole.
- Understanding complex problems and not being put off by difficult issues and challenges.
- Bringing strong conceptual and design skills to the team and pushing the team toward risk-taking behaviors.
- Initiating new ideas and starting new projects and activities.
- Looking to the future and creating vision for the organization.
- Serving as catalysts for quicker and more expansive change.

Leadership Style

As leaders, Originators:

- Are enthusiastic and energetic leaders.
- Are catalysts for changing the system.
- Provide the long-range vision for the organization and will, in fact, constantly revise the entire system.
- Conceptualize new systems, build new models and seek to be in charge of the start-up phase of any project.
- Prefer a unique leadership role to a more conventional one.
- Prefer to manage more than one task at a time.

Ineffective Originator Behavior

Ineffective Originators are the people with so many ideas that nothing productive ever gets done. They are the people who make decisions based solely on how an idea sounds to them. Their ideas and suggestions may not be realistic because they are presented without consideration for the context or the culture of the organization. Figuratively, they are the people whose enthusiasm for heating a house in a novel way results in burning it down. They might be Chernobyl's nuclear experimenters, who in 1986 violated operating regulations, standard precautions and safety rules, and ended up creating a nuclear disaster. They might be Bruce Ismay and Edward J. Smith, owner of White Star Lines and captain of the *Titanic*, respectively, who envisioned the largest, most luxurious and fastest way to cross the Atlantic. Ismay argued for an inadequate number of lifeboats in the interest of aesthetics and creature comforts. Smith ignored numerous warnings and many of the conventions of commanding a ship at sea to proceed full speed through dark, icy waters before striking an iceberg and sinking with the loss of approximately 1,500 lives.

Organizations want and need good ideas, but they have to give those ideas an opportunity to work to reap their benefits. Sometimes a leader, exhibiting characteristics of the ineffective Originator, will offer an innovation and then too quickly expect results. Behind the scenes, people may be working frantically to implement the innovation, struggling with very real and challenging obstacles and barriers. However, the innovative leader understands the world of ideas, not implementation. He or she may believe that the work is in the "thinking," so "why isn't it completed already." When they see that nothing has changed, they may conclude that their idea was not sufficiently innovative and produce another idea they see as even more innovative. This continuous disruption of effort can be disheartening and can lead to lower performance and commitment. In the end, none of the leader's ideas are implemented effectively and the organization finds that its performance has spiraled downward with each successive disruption. Well-intended employees are blamed for their lack of creativity and innovation. The frustrated leader is viewed as incompetent and with contempt by his or her employees. Even if the organization survives the downward spiral, its capacity to effectively implement change in the future has been seriously harmed.

Such incidents result from people with original and innovative ideas taking action, without awareness of their blind spots and without good counsel. A good idea poorly executed is a problem. An idea blindly promoted without due regard for the opinions of those who see matters differently is a mark of incompetence.

The following story illustrates an ineffective Originator. She has many creative and original ideas, but failure to focus on the most critical ones leads to the demise of the organization.

Case Study: Another Good Idea

"You know what I think would be great?" stated the executive director *in the regular Monday meeting in a manner that confirmed to everyone that she wasn't really asking a question. "I think we ought to connect all our computers in a local area network and then we'd have access to everybody's files."*

Nobody responded. Nobody ever did when she started with these unilateral brainstorms. No one else ever got a chance to talk. The meetings were always the same week after week. The director and founder of this educational nonprofit organization talked nonstop during every meeting. She rarely paused and no one else was ever directly asked to comment. Yet after listening to her own ideas nonstop for two hours (during which time she thought of at least six new ideas to add to last week's batch), she would feel energized and ready to tackle the work at hand. She had no concept of when enough was enough.

The staff would sit dumbfounded. They were bewildered and, in the end, discouraged. If anything was accomplished at all it was because they regrouped later in her absence and divided up the responsibilities for the project work and set priorities themselves. This included the writing of grant proposals to secure funding for the organization, contact with the volunteer leaders of the various chapters around the state, creation of articles for the "now-and-again" newsletter and researching future programs to be sponsored and produced. There were, in fact, a couple of dozen things going on at any one time and the executive director had an inconsistent hand in the middle of every one of them. She would forget what she had said previously and would reverse her decisions from one day to the next. She changed priorities on a whim. Her "start-stop-start again" style drained the energy and enthusiasm of the staff. In fact, the staff turned over continually as people who wanted to help but found that they could not, became frustrated and left the organization. Many projects were currently underway and the last thing the organization and the staff needed to be worrying about was connecting their hodge-podge of donated and out-dated computers into some sort of network. The office space was tiny and a "sneaker net" executed by walking disks from room to room was certainly not impractical.

The founder was charismatic. She had created this organization seemingly out of thin air and had been able to attract financial and advisory support from some notable citizens and institutions in the community. Members of the board now agreed that the organizational model could be rolled out to other states and replicated there. Her idea was celebrated and her accomplishments recognized in small but influential circles. She gladly took credit for what had been done in only a few years. She was also extremely intelligent and made factual connections and developed remarkable insights that eluded most other people. Her raw intellect was beyond reproach. However, what the organization needed now was a strategy and a process for establishing new chapters and for expanding membership. It also needed consistent internal operating policies and procedures. Although she continued to generate new ideas by the dozens and although many of them resulted in exciting, once-in-a-lifetime educational opportunities for some children, the organization did not grow in membership. Individual chapters declined and some folded. New chapters were not started and grant monies tied to the organization's growth were forfeited. For lack of adequate leadership and, perhaps because too many ideas were generated and too few were carried out, the organization declined and eventually closed its doors. Some thought it was a victim of its founder's unbridled creativity and her inability to stick to a plan of action. The founder concluded that nobody ever really understood her vision or what she was trying to accomplish.

Ineffective Originators tend to make impulsive decisions based on their sole perspectives without thinking through the consequences. For them, the excitement and satisfaction is in coming up with the original idea. They fail to grasp the complexities of implementation. They can see what the idea would look like if put into action, but they cannot master the processes required to bring the idea into sustainable existence.

Qualities of Ineffective Originators

Although a specific person may not exhibit all of these traits, this list helps describe in general the observable behaviors that can affect a group's efforts to produce collectively when led by an ineffective Originator. When leading a change effort, an ineffective Originator may:

- Jump from one idea to another.
- Make impulsive decisions.
- Fail to probe the consequences of change.
- Challenge organizational culture and norms with little regard or awareness for consequences.
- Not give a new idea enough time to be implemented before deciding to try something else.
- Believe that ideas have more value than outcomes.
- Get frustrated by questions that focus on details and implementation.
- Denigrate those who ask questions and label them as negative or as "resistors."

- Minimize the importance of relationships.
- Blame others when ideas are not enacted.
- Create chaos.

Potential Pitfalls for Originators

Each of the Change Styles is subject to potential problems and pitfalls that can lead to ineffective behaviors. Originators should be aware of their vulnerability to the following pitfalls:

- Originators may get carried away with their own creativity.
- Originators can sometimes become lost in theory, forget the current realities and overlook relevant details.
- Originators may ignore facts, logic and practical constraints that conflict with their vision or agenda.
- Originators may overextend themselves and ignore the impact their ideas have on the system and other people.
- Originators may not adapt well to new policies and procedures, especially when they add limitations that did not previously exist.
- Originators must guard against appearing unyielding in their positions and against discouraging others from challenging their ideas.
- Originators are at risk for moving on to new ideas and projects without completing those they have already started.

Prescriptive Remedies

To avoid style preference traps and to increase their flexibility, when anticipating or participating in a change effort, Originators should consider the following strategies:

- Try to see the situation the way a Conserver might. This can improve problem-solving and decision-making skills.

- Identify three things that are currently working. Identify five facts or individuals contributing to this success.
- Explore the history of the situation and understand the sequence of events that has led up to the problem or opportunity.
- Seek out someone you think is a Conserver and get their perspective. Only listen and ask questions. Remember, listening does not mean you agree.
- Try listing all the issues you imagine are important to Conservers.
- Wait to implement a new idea until you have had time to "sleep on it." This disrupts the automatic "well-of-course-it'll-work" decision mode and provides a safety valve for impulsivity.
- Resist the temptation to think aloud with the group. If necessary, brainstorm with someone prior to the meeting and bring your filtered ideas to the team.
- Make a list of relevant facts and details, and set realistic priorities and timelines. Ask a trusted colleague to provide feedback on your list.
- Assess the availability of resources before proceeding.
- Look at the impact of the decision on at least two other people and consider how it will affect someone important to you.
- Focus on the desired outcomes by creating a visual image that is as detailed as possible.
- Learn to assign priorities to activities to avoid being spread too thin and thus accomplishing nothing.
- Learn when to give up on an impractical idea and let other people be right.

Part Three

As we've seen in the previous sections, each of the three Change Styles can be executed effectively or ineffectively. Although the Change Styles themselves are neither right nor wrong, good nor bad, how one exhibits his or her Change Style Preference can create positive outcomes for the individual and the organization or it can create problems for both.

Being able to recognize the Change Style of others can give leaders a new tool for assessing potential contributions that can be made to an organization. Leaders can improve their own leadership effectiveness by taking specific actions to increase their sensitivity to the Change Styles of others. By doing so, they can help their organizations build flexibility and avoid certain traps inherent to each of the Change Style Preferences.

This final section will bring together what you've learned so far and help you do just that. In Chapters Eight and Nine, we will present two detailed case studies—*Dancing Beneath the Camel's Feet* and *No Good Deed Shall Go Unpunished*—to show Change Style Preferences at play in the interactions taking place within organizations. See if you can observe the effective and ineffective use of Change Styles. Many leaders find that after they learn how to differentiate among the three Change Styles, they can use these new lenses to look at daily situations inside their organizations. They can better understand the dynamics, opportunities and the challenges they face. And they become more effective leaders of more productive organizations. But first, they must learn to recognize the three Change Styles in action.

In Chapter Ten, we will draw on the concept of leader as artist to show you how to move more fluidly between Change Styles as the situation demands.

Chapter Eleven gives us a brief history of the best thinking on change over the past 50 years. This provides a context for our Change Process Model, which shows the four stages of change that everyone, no matter what their Change Style Preference, experiences. We expand this model to show the strengths and potential traps that may be experienced in each stage.

Finally, in Chapter Twelve, we bring it all together, giving managers specific, detailed do's and don'ts for every Change Style, every step of the way.

Chapter 8

DANCING BENEATH THE CAMEL'S FEET

Effective Use of Change Styles in the Odyssey of an Entrepreneur

In This Chapter

This story shows effective Originator behavior in a Conserver-dominated industry. This is the story of an original idea—its birth, its nurturance and its expression in the world at large. It is an idea that offers hope that medical science can soon address some of the most debilitating and tragic diseases of our day. The idea arose in one small division of a large, traditional company. Over several years, this innovative concept—this dream of improving the lot of mankind in some tangible way—was nurtured by the tenacious efforts of its unrelenting champion who was both an original thinker and a practical leader.

J. Donald deBethizy, PhD, President and CEO of Targacept, Inc., shares his experience as a successful innovator in a traditional company, while simultaneously building a collaboration between two very different industries.

Curious Connection

During the mid-'80s, Don deBethizy was hired as a senior toxicologist to work in the research and development area of a large tobacco company. The company had decided as part of its business strategy to learn as much as possible about nicotine chemistry, pharmacology and toxicology. He started as a bench scientist doing nicotine research on metabolism and pharmacokinetics. "In my early years, I was doing research and trying to make a reputation among my peers in the field," says deBethizy. "Our R&D department was almost like a research institute then. We were involved in the kind of research that most people never hear about—the kind that gets most of its attention among fellow researchers. We were good at publishing our work, but we had not yet developed any science that was leading to new products."

In the late '80s, it became apparent in the research community that cigarette smoking was somehow protecting people against Parkinson's and Alzheimer's diseases. Fewer smokers were subject to these diseases than nonsmokers. Some 20 studies had been accumulated in each disease area and all the researchers agreed that something was going on that appeared to be neuroprotective. Scientists hypothesized that it involved a nicotinic cholinergic process.

The normal neurotransmitter in the body is called acetylcholine (ACh), which happens to act on two receptors. They are both ACh receptors, but they are very different. One was characterized during one hundred years of research on the pharmacology of nicotine. The other was characterized by the use of another plant product called muscarine. Consequently, medical terminology adopted the terms "nicotinic" and "muscarinic" in identifying these two distinct classes of ACh receptors.

The tobacco company's research centered on the nicotinic ACh receptor. For a hundred years, scientists have known that these nicotinic ACh receptors have acted as binding sites for nicotine in the brain, but it was not until molecular biology techniques were developed in the mid-1980s that scientists were able to characterize the genes involved. They discovered the processes that cause these receptors to open and thereby allow conductance of sodium and calcium ions, depolarizing the nerve cell membrane. That finding meant that scientists could potentially develop medicines that would target only certain parts of the brain where they were needed. Such chemicals targeted to particular receptors in the brain would reduce the side effects caused by stimulating all nicotinic ACh receptors as nicotine does.

In the late '80s, interest was growing in the cholinergic receptor and its potential for treating diseases such as Alzheimer's. Recognizing the potential for development, in 1990 the head of R&D decided to form a pharmacology group. All the nicotine researchers—PhD-level pharmacologists, toxicologists and chemists—were brought together with deBethizy as manager. Their mission was to become the world's leading authority on nicotine. The highly prolific team produced about 300 research papers and abstracts.

Patent Pending

But research was just the start of the plan. Soon they began patenting previously discovered molecular compounds for specific therapeutic uses. "We started patenting these molecules for particular uses, for neuro-degenerative diseases," said deBethizy. "In hindsight, that was a very clever thing to do because it carved out an early patent position for us. It also helped us transition from an academically focused group to an organization with a commercial mission. The tobacco company senior executives were receptive to this new commercial focus, because they were used to seeing products manufactured and sold."

In 1992, a former vice president of an international consumer products firm became the new head of R&D. The involvement of someone from the consumer products area was invigorating for the R&D team. He recognized the company's research efforts on nicotine as something worthwhile. He appreciated deBethizy's enthusiasm and championed this research to the tobacco company's CEO.

No Smoking

Another opportunity soon arose through other tobacco company connections. An Asian tobacco company—a government-owned monopoly—had formed a pharmaceutical company. With close to a billion dollars invested, they were interested in nicotine for treating diseases. "They brought over a fully developed collaborative plan completely finished and handed it to us," says deBethizy. "We were astonished. They were proposing some challenging science but needed some help. They just knew from a business perspective that this was an unexploited therapeutic target with high commercial potential. Over the next two years, our scientists collaborated with them on pharmaceutical research. However, at the end of this time, the pharmaceutical company decided to pursue its own technology."

Smoke and Mirrors

Meanwhile, R&D continued to explore the "business of science." They wanted to achieve a level of independence for their operations by becoming less of a cost center for the larger organization. Because R&D wanted to generate about 25 percent of its budget from outside sources, it formed a business development team called the New Business Group to explore the commercial potential of some of the company's technology.

"It was a great idea but ahead of its time," recalls deBethizy. "The business units of the company were not ready for it because the core tobacco business was so profitable. There was no need to do anything different."

However, this focus of R&D on new business development provided an environment for expanding the commercial focus of the patented portfolio of compounds. "I was wondering how to proceed about this time," says deBethizy, "when I went to talk to the head of R&D. He said, 'Don, you can't wait for the perfect compound. Pick one and start developing it.' My team chose #2403. It wasn't the ideal compound and it wasn't novel, but it was our best one and we had patent protection for its use to treat diseases like Alzheimer's. His advice was the best I ever received because it stimulated us to take risks with the technology we had."

When the New Business Group formed a New Business Council to rank the best technologies in R&D for further development, deBethizy took a risk and put forward the nicotine program as the first one to be evaluated. "About this time," recalls deBethizy, "the nicotine patch had been introduced and some researchers were treating diseases with it. There was growing clinical data showing that nicotine was effective in treating Tourette's syndrome. At the first meeting of the New Business Council, we showed a video of an adolescent boy being treated for Tourette's with a single nicotine patch. It was like watching the movie *Awakenings*. Suddenly the boy's ticks and barks disappeared. The demonstration made a powerful point. We got $800,000 that day to do the preclinical safety assessment and Phase I clinical trials on compound #2403—critical first steps along the drug development path. The New Business Council could see the commercial value in these nicotinic compounds as pharmaceuticals. They recognized that taking #2403 through Phase I clinical trials would significantly raise the commercial value of the portfolio."

Walking a Tightrope

About this time, the Tobacco Wars were heating up and the Federal Drug Administration was clamoring to have tobacco regulated as a drug. Tobacco companies were being accused of "spiking" the cigarettes with added nicotine to make them more addictive. On a daily basis, executives and company spokesmen were defending the tobacco companies against such accusations.

"Here I was working on pharmaceutical applications of nicotine-related compounds," says deBethizy, "while the tobacco company was arguing with the FDA over whether nicotine in tobacco should be regulated as a drug. There was a great deal of concern among the senior executives about the impact of our fledgling pharmaceutical initiative on the company's position toward nicotine and tobacco. But I was able to keep talking about it in such a way to emphasize that nicotine was a drug only under certain unique circumstances. In the end, that worked in our favor.

"During this time, I was a spokesman for the tobacco company on technical matters relating to nicotine and even appeared in an interview on ABC's *Day One*. I was a soldier and an officer in the field in the Tobacco Wars, but in the midst of all that, I had to keep this pharmaceutical concept alive. If I hadn't kept pushing, it may very well have been shut down completely because it was too confusing to a lot of people in the tobacco business."

Drug Deals

In 1996, deBethizy engaged a consultant to help the R&D team find a pharmaceutical company to create a partnership around compound #2403. The consultant helped the R&D team converge their thinking and prepared them to approach potential partners. The team finished the preclinical and

Phase I clinical studies, revised its research plan and formed a subsidiary called Targacept in 1997. The name came from "targeted receptors" which was, in its simplest terms, a description of its business.

"The tobacco company had never done a clinical trial before," said deBethizy. "After all, we were not a pharmaceutical company. We ran into some difficulty internally but it was mostly people just trying to do their jobs of protecting the company. For example, the liability insurance covering the tobacco company did not protect the company against liability incurred during clinical trials. To get around that hurdle, we purchased a special rider for this kind of coverage."

With the clinical trials completed, Targacept sent letters of inquiry to 70 pharmaceutical companies and received invitations from 68 to present compound #2403 and the nicotinic program. "Our compound had a use patent that we learned 'Big Pharma' doesn't like," recalls deBethizy. "The compound was rapidly metabolized and there wasn't much residual drug left in the blood. We learned very quickly that our compound was not exactly what they wanted. They wanted a compound that offered once-a-day dosing in pill form that had tremendous efficacy, no side effects and measurable blood levels. Those are the rules they play by. If you want in, you meet their expectations."

"Our consultant had recommended that we spin out the company and completely separate the technology from the tobacco company. But I rejected that because at the time I wanted to transform the tobacco company. I believed there was a broad spectrum of product opportunities from nicotinic therapies to nicotine replacement products to reduced-risk cigarettes. I thought there was a big opportunity to use our technology in several new arenas. But I couldn't sell that vision. I worked on it for a long time, four years actually. Of course, I recognize now how grandiose that was—trying to change a hundred-year-old tobacco company."

Headwind

At the beginning of 1997, the cast of characters changed in the seats of power at the tobacco company. The head of R&D left and a new CEO ascended. No longer did deBethizy have people at the top championing his project. He was facing a headwind for the first time. "The new CEO was a real operations-oriented, bottom-line kind of guy," says deBethizy. "I had to understand that, step up and take the entire responsibility for moving Targacept forward. That was tough, because I basically risked my entire career at this point by championing a non-core-business in an environment of declining resources."

"The tobacco company was cutting budgets in all departments and I found myself arguing for a larger piece of a shrinking pie. I made some enemies, I'm afraid. Those who didn't see the same potential as I did attacked the program. Many on the R&D management team thought the nicotinic opportunity was 'off-purpose.' In fact, I was dealing with a lot of Myers-Briggs personality type ISTJs and ESTJs. SJ's[1] tend to be stronger Conservers than any of the other Myers-Briggs profiles. They are very much oriented to the bottom line. And that's where I got misread.

"Sometimes I may seem to be off-purpose and to have a great deal of enthusiasm for things that don't seem like they will bear fruit. However, I have a good sense of what is possible and I can stay focused on a long-term goal in the face of adversity. I have learned that by surrounding myself with people who can focus on completing near-term tasks and producing results, the vision gets delivered. And that's where I've made a difference with Targacept. I always addressed the concerns that were expressed. I figured out what they wanted: science, deals and patents. Once I learned that, we delivered it on a regular basis. That's the business of science and my team was good at it. But the executives at the tobacco company reminded me every day that our team was not yet creating any product or any sales. I just had to remind myself continually that the products would come in due course."

Into 1997, Targacept was presenting its science to several potential partners, all of whom were very interested. One early opportunity looked quite promising, but fell apart late in negotiations for reasons that had nothing to do with the technology's credibility or the viability of the business plan.

"I was devastated by losing a very good deal with a major U.S. pharmaceutical company," says deBethizy. "I'd been saying we were going to deliver a deal that would bring money into R&D. Bringing in money to make Targacept self-supporting was the only way that we were going to keep the dream alive this time. We were at the end of our rope. The one selling feature I could offer the CEO and his bottom-line orientation was the promise of money which would validate the science we'd already created. And now the deal I'd promised was dead.

"I told the CEO I could resurrect all the other leads we had looked at previously and get a deal, if he'd let me have until the end of the year to close on it. He took a risk on me and the team. He gave us that additional time to find a deal."

Huffing and Puffing

During that summer, Targacept worked hard to make compound #2403 even more attractive to potential partners. The scientists modified the compound to create a novel compound and submitted a patent. They designed the compound, synthesized it and tested it in only four months. Meanwhile Targacept's detractors inside the tobacco company were reveling in the team's failure to secure the pharmaceutical deal they had promised.

"This was a tough time for us," says deBethizy. "I had to buoy the Targacept team's morale and keep my detractors at bay. They were saying, 'I told you so. Don is just a dreamer who can shoot a line of bull.' This was where my natural orientation toward optimism and enthusiasm for what's possible made me vulnerable. My detractors emphasized those qualities as negatives rather than championing them as strengths in the R&D organization. I still had powerful allies, but their support was waning. So there it was. I was risking my career as a scientist over Targacept because it allowed me to be characterized as off-purpose."

Building Another Head of Steam

By the fall of 1998, Targacept had completed its revision of compound #2403 and was focusing on talks with two new pharmaceutical firms. One was quite interested but was going through a merger with another company at the time. Matters got complicated but a deal looked promising. But in early December of 1998, the merging company had bowed out.

"I was in Europe when I got the word that one of two prospective partners was no longer a candidate. I remember it was Pearl Harbor Day. I felt like I'd been bombed. Here it was, December 7, and I still didn't have a deal. I'd promised the CEO I'd have one by year-end and the 31st was getting closer. Fortunately, I'd listened to some good advice. We had a separate negotiation running in parallel with a second company. We just focused on them. They knew we were talking with another company, we just never told them that the other company was now out of consideration.

"From London, Targacept brought into its camp the top biotech attorney in the world to work on the agreement. He and his associate drafted the agreement but we did not get a term sheet signed by both parties. That meant that the contract negotiation would have to address all the issues usually contained in the term sheet. That lead the two parties into round-the-clock negotiations in Philadelphia just before Christmas. After two-and-a-half days, they broke until after the holidays."

Done Deal

"During the break in negotiations for Christmas, I sat down and mapped out the deal on a huge sheet of paper. It was my first big pharmaceutical deal, but I knew what Targacept needed, and what we had to give up didn't seem that bad. Besides, December 31 was approaching and I had to have a deal to keep my promise to the CEO. Of course, I was the only one who knew about that time limit. I couldn't tell anyone and I couldn't even let it show in my body language. So I went against the advice I was getting from well-meaning people and went back to Philadelphia. We had another round of negotiations around-the-clock, no sleep. We talked, we argued, we postured, but in the end we signed the deal at 11:00 P.M. on December 31. Believe me, I know the meaning of 'eleventh-hour interventions.' And it was a great deal, too—one that any start-up company would love to have. Afterwards, we went over to the bar at the Ritz Carlton and drank a bottle of champagne to celebrate not only the new year but a new beginning."

The news of a deal and a kept promise was well received at headquarters. The tobacco executives were excited. It seemed to them that sums of cash would soon be coming in the door. But skeptics still abounded. After all, no products were actually being produced and nothing as yet was being sold. Knowing that, the CEO had some key advice for deBethizy. He said, "Show me the money, Don. You've got to deliver on this pharmaceutical deal. If you focus exclusively on that and succeed, then that reputation will allow you to do other things."

"That was great advice for me," deBethizy recalls, "because I got really focused on making this deal a success. But I knew we had to do more as well.

"My view was that we should go out and find partners for all the other molecules we had for other diseases, based on what we were doing in this new partnership with 'Big Pharma' and based on all the data we had for Alzheimer's and

Parkinson's diseases. We tried that, but 'Big Pharma' wanted to see our compounds in their own disease models. They needed to see preclinical data showing that the compounds that we had were appropriate to their applications. We just didn't have the data."

Fire in the Hole

Research interest on neuronal nicotinic (ACh) receptors was starting to increase. Targacept had competition. In fact, our "Big Pharma" partner had selected Targacept over a competing biotech company. Going to the senior executives at the tobacco company, deBethizy said Targacept needed more money to get the preclinical data on these other diseases to secure these other deals. "I said, 'I need $12 million,'" recalled deBethizy. "I didn't expect to get it, and my detractors now had new ammunition. They reminded the CEO that originally I'd thought we wouldn't need any more money. Now here we were asking for more money—money that the tobacco company didn't have. I just had to sit there and take the verbal abuse. That's the way I had to deal with my critics. If I'd blown up and left, it would have been over. So I just listened until they calmed down, and then I disagreed with them and gave them the facts."

The tobacco company and Targacept agreed to seek venture capital to finance the research that was needed and also as a way to validate with knowledgeable investors whether Targacept could be a sustainable business. "In the process, our staff learned something about how the financial markets would value the business. We also learned about the stipulations that would accompany a venture capital investment, such as a minority ownership position for the tobacco company, a neutral board and an experienced CEO." By March, three international investors were syndicated through International Biotechnology Trust (IBT), headquartered in London. The necessary work to separate Targacept from the tobacco company got underway. Although work proceeded into the spring, the investors missed two proposed closing dates at the ends of April and May. In June, unfortunately, IBT experienced a stockholder revolt due to low share price and all pending deals were put on hold. Targacept faced yet another hurdle. Fortunately it had been working with another venture capitalist as a potential lead, Euclid SR, and offered them the deal if they could complete it by July 31.

"They said 'yes.' Of course they knew (and we knew) they couldn't do the deal that fast, but it showed us how much they wanted the deal," said deBethizy. "But there was still this issue of who should be CEO. The investors needed me in the company, but they wanted an experienced CEO. I thought about acquiescing and taking the position of president, but I still thought I was the best person to run the company. I also knew our investors were benchmarking our company against another biotech investment they had in agribusiness, a spin-off from Novartis. I checked into it and learned that the CEO was a guy just like me, an R&D administrator with a science background who had spun out the company. I made the issue a deal-breaker. The investors and the parent company decided I would be CEO. That put everyone in the position of helping me be successful. We spun out Targacept on August 24, 2000."

On Fire

So the question now is, "Is the work finished or just beginning?" "We've got a lot of work to do because we're transforming into a product-focused pharmaceutical company," said deBethizy. "We're fortunate to have the deals with the pharmaceutical industry. We're meeting the developmental milestones for our deals and developing products in Lewy body dementia, pain, depression, Tourette's syndrome, anxiety and schizophrenia. Business is definitely picking up."

Conclusion

Targacept started as an idea arising in one small part of a large, established and successful tobacco company. Over several years the idea was nurtured by the tenacious efforts of one unrelenting champion, an Originator at heart. Using his Pragmatist skills, he picked his way carefully through the Conserver-oriented corporate world. He did not want to have his dream crushed beneath the unwieldy and plodding feet of the ambling corporate behemoth of which he was a part. Eventually Targacept escaped from underfoot. Now that it is outside the tobacco company and the tobacco industry, these innovators find themselves facing both familiar and different challenges in an entirely new industry, pharmaceuticals, another Conserver-oriented world. Targacept hopes to prove that in that environment, nimble and creative companies open to change can indeed thrive and survive while dancing in between the measured steps of another species of lumbering giant.

Notes

[1] deBethizy's intuition about the relationship between the Myers-Briggs Type Indicator and Change Style Indicator was accurate. SJs (Sensing Judgers) are the strongest Conservers. Sixty-five percent of ISFJs are Conservers, as are 56 percent of ISTJs. NPs (Intuitive Perceivers) are the strongest Originators. Fifty-five percent of ENTPs are Originators, as are 52 percent of INTPs. Current norms for Change Style Indicator by Myers-Briggs Type Indictor, profession/function, industry and gender are available at Discovery Learning's Web site at no charge (www.discoverylearning.com).

Chapter 9

NO GOOD DEED SHALL GO UNPUNISHED

Ineffective Use of Change Styles in Another Dot-com Disaster

In This Chapter

Here we will see how an Originator-heavy organization with great ideas and intentions floundered without established systems and realistic money-making methods. A group of collaborators launched a new dot-com, expanded its offering of services and faced the demanding expectations of both medical and investment professionals. It is a story about courage, conviction and greed, but above all, it is a story about change.

During the go-go days of Internet expansion in the late 1990s, business-to-consumer Web sites were all the rage. At the peak of the financing frenzy, dot-com millionaires were created overnight as investors threw buckets of money at fledgling companies. It seemed that everyone was attempting to get in on the ground floor of "the next big thing." In this environment, many ideas, some better than others, were funded with exorbitant sums of investment capital.

Offering his own idea for an Internet-based business, former U.S. Surgeon General Dr. C. Everett Koop joined with entrepreneurs Don Hackett and John Zacarro to fulfill Koop's vision as a public health professional of increasing each individual's responsibility for managing his or her own health care. Although neither Hackett nor Zacarro had strong business backgrounds, together these entrepreneurs launched a high-profile Web site that provided health information services they believed the public needed and wanted. To finance the rapid expansion of the site, they took the company public and made an initial public offering (IPO) of the company's stock. Despite Dr. Koop's well-intentioned prescription for what ailed the delivery of health care in America, this specific combination of remedies turned out to be toxic. As financial expectations of investors increased, drkoop.com was in danger of succumbing to the fate that befell many other dot-coms in the "technology crash of 2000."

Good for What Ails You

His vision was grand and noble, and nothing short of a revolution: To change entirely the way health care was delivered in this country. Dr. C. Everett Koop, former Surgeon General under President Reagan, had spent six decades in the medical profession and still saw, perhaps more clearly than anyone else, the need to change the current system for delivering health care in America. Dr. Koop's attitude about changes in American health care was captured in the following quote.

"There is no question that the idea of community in medicine is new. Just a decade ago, it was somewhat different and a generation ago it was entirely different. Back then, medicine and health were very private things. You did not develop communities; in fact, the last thing you wanted was a community talking about your health problems.

"The Internet makes community development very easy, but it also could never have developed as rapidly as it did had it not been for the fact that the self-help movement had already started to break down the barriers about talking about health problems—not so much about diagnosis or treatment aspects, but about how to manage the problems that go with it.

"The first thing to remember is that doctors, in general, like a well-informed patient because they can skip all the preliminaries and use a vocabulary that is understood by the patient without having to resort to simplistic talk.

"I'm a firm believer that the more a patient knows, the better the health care is in that community because the doctor has to rise to that level" (Scoop: Hang' with Dr. Koop, 1999, p. 15).

In his eighties, Dr. Koop remained an energetic visionary with strong beliefs about how to help the greatest number of people. He believed in the ability of individuals to take personal initiative and control their own health care. His philosophy was simple: Knowledge is the best prescription. His message was clear: "You take charge of your own health [especially now with managed care] because if you don't nobody else will" (Scoop: Hang' with Dr. Koop, p. 15). His tool of choice was the most logical: becoming a business-to-consumer dot-com portal on the Internet. The powerful engine for driving this venture would be the cash provided by an initial public offering (IPO).

The Vision

In 1997, Dr. Koop had begun working to perfect and promote an idea that would empower individuals to invest in monitoring and managing their own health care. With partners Don Hackett and John Zacarro, he had begun developing a software product called Dr. Koop's Personal Medical Record

System. With access to this software tool, individuals could store their personal medical records, their current list of prescriptions and whom to contact in an emergency. Dr. Koop also envisioned that in the future doctors could report the results of lab work and examinations directly to this record. But some observers wondered if consumers who were pressed for time and concerned about privacy would actually take the time to enter information into the software.

By the middle of the following year, business-to-consumer dot-coms were flourishing. The three partners recognized the opportunity to bring this idea to the broadest number of people and to augment it with additional medical- and health-related information. At the time, over 15,000 health-related portals could be found on the Internet, but the partners recognized the value of having Dr. Koop associated with their effort. They felt confident that with the help of health care professionals who were experienced in communications media and a focused effort in marketing, they could attract Web traffic that would entice advertisers whose fees would support the venture.

Nancy Snyderman, MD, a surgeon and medical correspondent for ABC, was invited to join with Dr. Koop in making his idea a reality. Serving as a member of the Medical Advisory Board and reflecting on her association with drkoop.com, she said, "The reason I joined was because of my experience as a communicator in very traditional media—television and radio. I knew that the Internet was the next logical step and that if we could integrate all those things, so much the better. I'd known Dr. Koop a long time and knew him to be a wonderful, ethical person, so I eagerly joined because of him. My job was to be an idea person at board meetings. I was to look at ways we could move to incorporate traditional and not-so-traditional communication media. Also, I was to help coordinate some of the data that went on the Web, review some articles and write some material as well."[1]

By early 1999, drkoop.com was receiving one million visitors a month (Schwartz & Boitano, 2000, p. 156). What was needed now was cash for promoting and advertising the new Web site.

The Money

Don Hackett believed that taking the company public was the most efficient way to raise the capital they needed. Dr. Koop agreed, noting that he had tried unsuccessfully to promote his personal medical record concept through nonprofit efforts. Now, he believed, a for-profit venture, especially one that could benefit from the high valuation of Internet start-ups, was the solution. Drkoop.com approached several investment bankers and in a matter of months, Bear, Stearns & Company was taking the venture public. In the *Wall Street Journal,* Dr. Koop was quoted as saying:

> "A for-profit venture . . . was probably the last opportunity I'd have to get my message across. I realized the only way to do it on the Internet was to make money through advertising. I jumped on that like a trout to a fly" (Carrns, 2000, p. B1).

Bear, Stearns & Company was eager to get the business and may have outbid more experienced and perhaps more prudent firms. They wanted this high-profile offering to gain exposure in the tech sector. An experienced banker, Bill Benedetto took exception to their optimism about the venture's potential and readiness. "All it had was a brand name and it looked flimsy. But then a lot of the deals looked pretty flimsy, because no one was asking whether they should be sold in the first place" (Schwartz & Boitano, 2000, p. 156). Even though some thought Bear Stearns a little reckless in underwriting drkoop.com, others such as Bill McGahan, an investment banker in another firm, conceded, "Health care was seen as a huge opportunity on the Web, and a whole bunch of companies were moving into this space. Going public was the way you got a foothold" (Schwartz & Boitano, p. 156).

At $9 a share, the IPO raised $84 million dollars, as investors eager to get in on "the next big thing" bid up the stock value on day one to $16. This was not atypical in the frenzied financing of dot-coms; nevertheless, some voiced concerns. Stephen DeNelsky, an experienced e-health analyst, thought it was quite early in the venture's life for it to be going public. At this point, drkoop.com had existed for only a few months and had less than a million dollars lifetime revenue, yet here it was capitalized at $84 million. "I couldn't get comfortable with the company's revenue projections," said DeNelsky. "I just thought it was premature" (Schwartz & Boitano, p. 156).

The Operation

The business plan was to attract visitors to the site who wanted reliable information and to sell advertising to companies who wanted to sell their products and services to those who frequented the site. In concept, it was no different from selling advertising on television, radio or in magazines. Users would be attracted to content and advertisers would be attracted to the users. But there was a difference. Consumers were experienced with these established media and were sophisticated enough to distinguish information from advertising. The Internet was new to everyone. Many were uncertain what to make of the information that could be found there and how to know which was reliable. The barriers for participating in this medium were low. Almost anyone could establish a Web site. Useless and erroneous information was everywhere. Consumers were looking for someone they could trust. Again, Dr. Koop's reputation swayed investors and users alike.

At the beginning of 1999, health information was the hottest topic on the Internet (after sex, of course). A Harris Poll showed that 60 million Americans had gone on-line in

1998 to get health-related information. In the summer of 1999, drkoop.com was receiving 3.2 million visits per month to its site, displaying 66,000 separate pages of content (Stoneham, 1999, p. 29). The marketing director of the venture, Guy MacNeill, declared that drkoop.com would distinguish itself as the premier health care information Web site by carrying out its "4-C" strategy—content, community, cool tools and commerce. Content was deemed the most important and was the driver for the Web site. Breaking stories on health care news were updated three times daily. Drkoop.com signed a deal with ABC Multimedia, Inc., to be the health channel for its ABC LocalNet programs. Drkoop.com also provided health care content to Web sites for 100 ABC affiliate stations.

In addition to content, the "cool tools" were an attraction to users. Enabling visitors to evaluate their life-styles' impacts on longevity and to check for potential negative effects from the interaction of up to 16 concurrent prescription drugs with the Drug Checker tool were just some of the valued tools on the site. The community aspect was a major attraction to users as well. One hundred support communities met on-line weekly to share information about their personal experiences with health issues. This feature was close to making Dr. Koop's vision a reality. Unfortunately, this was not the part of the 4-C strategy that would most satisfy the investors. That burden fell on commerce (Stoneham, p. 29).

The commerce component of the strategy was a little more difficult to enact. Strategic e-commerce partnerships were established with prominent drugstore Web sites, Phar-Mor and Drug Emporium. These partnerships allowed drkoop.com visitors to purchase their prescriptions on-line and to have access to 20,000 products. Other commercial concepts developed as organizations approached drkoop.com with ideas to cooperate and capitalize on what many believed would be the dominant health care information Web site.

Regardless of how the money was being made, management at drkoop.com knew they needed to promote the Web site and to attract more visitors. They made two highly publicized and strategic deals for distribution of their Web site. During the heady, early days of the venture, they agreed to pay Disney's Go Network nearly $58 million over three years to be the exclusive provider of health care information on that Network. Obviously drkoop.com management was anticipating development of substantial revenues from their operations. Shortly after the IPO, when they were flush with cash, management agreed to pay $89 million over four years to be featured (but not exclusively) on the AOL Web site. That last deal represented more than all the capital raised by the IPO and threw up some red flags for a few observers about the business acumen of those running drkoop.com. Indeed, the company was losing money hand over fist while revenues climbed only slightly. In the six months following the IPO, drkoop.com had spent $50 million while raising revenues of only $8 million (Schwartz & Boitano, p. 156).

Criticism of Ethics

The business model for drkoop.com involved charging a fee for placing advertisements on its Web site. This was the standard arrangement for business-to-consumer Web sites at the time. Unfortunately, the staff's enthusiasm for selling advertising and the attendant promotional claims made on behalf of the advertisers in their placement on the Web pages caused a furor over Dr. Koop's ethics. Hospitals who simply paid a fee to be listed were called "the most innovative and advanced health care institutions across the country" (Sherrid, 1999, p. 51). Another arrangement involved revenue generated for drkoop.com whenever someone referred from the Web site enrolled in a clinical trial program for a certain pharmaceutical company. Criticism of such flagrant combinations of information and advertising and undisclosed financial arrangements was loud and caustic. It came from several quarters.

Dr. Arthur Caplan, Director of the Center for Bioethics at the University of Pennsylvania Health System, stated: "The current tempest over the drkoop.com Web site is revealing not so much about Dr. Koop's own ethics but about the lack of ethical consensus concerning medicine on the Internet. It is very important that those who use the Internet know when conflicts of interest exist, what financial ties are present and who is vetting the accuracy of information . . . Most of the Web sites now operating will, and should, address the issue of how to keep editorial credibility in an age of big money and high stakes" (Charatan, 1999, p. 727).

Dr. Koop's response was, "I have never been bought. I cannot be bought. I am an icon and I have a reputation for honesty and integrity" (Charatan, p. 727).

A Plague of Mistakes

Any new enterprise will make more than its fair share of mistakes, but as several philosophers have noted in so many words: "That which does not kill us makes us stronger." Unfortunately, the mistakes drkoop.com was making were bordering on lethal.

Operating in a fishbowl enterprise where everyone was on display, every action that raised an eyebrow was a potential death knell for the company's credibility. One month after the IPO, several executives had to announce and explain that family members had sold shares of their stock prior to the end of the six-month holding period. These SEC violations were rectified by a swift return of proceeds to the company but not without embarrassment to key members of the organization and not without raising the specter of profiteering by insiders. Later when the hold on stock (known as the "lockup") was released, several key executives did sell large blocks of their stock. The markets saw this move as indicative of management trouble, although Dr. Koop declared that his sales were simply to meet philanthropic commitments. Rumors surfaced about pending changes in management. The stock continued to slide in value as revenues for the first quarter of 2000 were below internal projections.

The original partnership involved a handful of people but, after the IPO, the company swelled to 150 employees. Drkoop.com occupied 80,000 square feet of office space in Austin with a lease running to 2006. The office was full of twenty-something employees and purple beanbag chairs. The entire atmosphere was upscale, hip and expensive. Money was flowing out of the organization in orders of magnitude greater than that which was coming in. The business model for business-to-consumer dot-coms was failing and coming under scrutiny all across the infant Internet industry. By the spring of 2000, investors were concerned about seeing no return on their investments. Stock values plummeted and with them the reputations of high-profile visionaries like Dr. Koop were becoming tarnished.

Diagnosis: Ailing Organization

As the business situation for drkoop.com declined, its accountant, PricewaterhouseCoopers LLC, felt obliged to express doubts about the ability of the organization to continue as a growing concern. They did so in a note to their form 10K filed in 1999 with the Securities and Exchange Commission (*DrKoop.com Prospects Dim*, 2000, p. 36). The stock price declined further amidst investor disenchantment with "content" Web sites that relied on revenue from advertisers.

After the NASDAQ crash of April 14, 2000, visitors to drkoop.com declined from 3.5 million different visitors in March to half that in May. For the same month, rival site WebMD.com had 6 million different visitors and OnHealth.com had over 5 million. Responding to the decline in stock value and the declining revenue, drkoop.com cut its employee count by 35 percent, letting 52 employees go. In July, two class action lawsuits were filed against management alleging the withholding of financial information for the purpose of propping up its stock price. That same month, two top executives, the chief operations officer and the chief financial officer, resigned. In August, the stock fell below $1 a share.

In late August 2000, drkoop.com received a life-saving cash infusion of $20 million from new investors and a new CEO, Richard Rosenblatt. Rosenblatt was an executive of Prime Ventures, one of the new investors, and formerly had been an executive of Excite@Home and CEO of iMall; he had credible experience in the dot-com industry. He said, "We're exploring a lot of different avenues and we'll do whatever it takes to maximize shareholder value. If that means we run the company, sell it or acquire companies, we'll do whatever it takes. We're realists" (Bronstad, 2000, p. 24).

Conclusion

An old saying declares, "If you build a better mousetrap, the world will beat a path to your door." In the speculative e-commerce economy of the late 1990s, it seems that simply promising to build a better mousetrap was enough to create a stampede of wealthy investors to the doorsteps of creative, but untested, innovators. This was the environment that greatly rewarded many original thinkers for their concepts and forward thinking. But after the honeymoon was over, the practicality of many ventures was tested by the traditional expectations of the financial markets that demanded profits and positive business performance.

One observer, Douglas Henton, president of Collaborative Economics, offered this: "Call it old fashioned, but at some point, these companies had to start making money. This has been a healthy shakeout in which some companies fail and others refine themselves" (Nasri, 2000, p. 10817). Market conditions encouraged rapid expansion, especially in the technology sector. In many situations the expansion was not balanced with adequate infrastructure and a solid foundation.

The dot-com companies of the late '90s, were full of Originators with great ideas and willingness to take risks. Cutting-edge technology and a hungry market sparked rapid growth and expansion. However, to be sustainable the dot-coms also needed the contributions of Conservers and Pragmatists, such as infrastructure, well-integrated operating systems and the ability to adapt as lessons were learned.

The dot-com expansion of the late '90s is metaphorically similar to trees that grow rapidly under ideal weather conditions. From the outside the trees appear green and healthy. However their support systems (roots and trunk) are underdeveloped to support the tree's crown under less than ideal circumstances. Once weather conditions change, trees that have grown rapidly will die in the slightest drought or topple under the lightest wind. And so it is with enterprises that are founded by Originators who lack the understanding of the need for substance, infrastructure and measurable outcomes. Their focus may be entirely on growth and expansion without any awareness of the need for coordination and integration.

Notes

[1] Interview with Nancy Snyderman, MD on Oct. 20, 2000. Dr. Snyderman was a medical correspondent and reporter for ABC and a member of the board of directors of drkoop.com.

Chapter 10

THE ART OF CHANGE

Creativity and the Change Style Continuum

"It takes working in all three dimensions of the Change Style continuum to be a successful artist. Every painter is a chemist; every sculptor, an engineer."

Cheryl DeCiantis

In This Chapter

L eaders of successful change initiatives are creators. Their approach to change resembles the approaches used by successful artists. Max De Pree, former CEO of Herman Miller and author of *The Art of Leadership,* explores leadership as more art than science. He describes leadership as "something to be learned over time, not simply by reading books. Leadership is more tribal than scientific, more a weaving of relationships than an amassing of information, and, in that sense, I don't know how to pin it down in every detail" (De Pree, 1998, p. 3). Leader as artist is a provocative metaphor.

To successfully lead change you must demonstrate flexibility, self-awareness, empathy for others and willingness to stretch beyond your comfort zone.

This chapter will explore:

- The difference between creativity and creating.
- Key concepts of effective change leadership.
- Knowing when and how to work outside of your style.
- Working with people who can help you work out of your style or comfort zone.

Cheryl DeCiantis— Teaching the Art of Leadership[1]

Leadership consultant Cheryl DeCiantis teaches leaders. She is also an accomplished artist. She paints, sculpts and constructs three-dimensional objects that have meaning, aesthetic appeal and mathematical elegance. She expresses and interprets meaning through diverse media and knows both the history and regimen of a variety of art forms. She can visualize the expression of her thoughts and feelings, and she also understands in great detail the mechanics of the media she uses. Bringing together her creative ideas with attention to technique and detail, she produces art that others can see, touch and appreciate.

DeCiantis is also familiar with the Change Style model from her years of work as Artist in Residence at the Center for Creative Leadership. She also served for a number of years as the director of the European Campus of the Center for Creative Leadership in Brussels. In the expression of her artistic talents, DeCiantis moves across the Change Style continuum using the perceptions and behaviors of the three styles as they are needed. "It takes working in all three dimensions of the Change Style continuum to be a successful artist," she declares. "Every painter is a chemist; every sculptor, an engineer."

As an Originator, she first generates a concept. From her Conserver side, she understands the tools and process of a chosen art form and their limits. As a Pragmatist, she brings the skills and ideas together to create a physical expression of what she has envisioned.

DeCiantis is also uniquely gifted in her ability to lead individuals in the discovery of their own creativity. At the Center for Creative Leadership, she conducted numerous workshops designed to help business leaders unlock and discover their creative nature. In the process she helped them understand the two essential skills required to manage change effectively: *flexibility* and *empathy*. To arrive at those conclusions, her students focused on other lessons first.

Creativity vs. Creating

An essential first step to functioning as an effective leader is to understand the difference between *creativity* and *creating*. Creativity is the process of thinking or imagining unique and novel ideas. Creating is the process of bringing those ideas into reality. From this perspective, creativity becomes a subset of creating. "Ideas alone are not enough," DeCiantis reminds her workshop participants. "They are necessary, but as every leader knows you've got to put those ideas into motion and make them reality." Quite often the latter step requires a set of skills and a way of looking at the world that is different from the skills and perspective of the visionary idea generator.

Robert Fritz, in *The Path of Least Resistance*, divides the dynamics of creating into three aspects. The first is to acknowledge and communicate "current reality." Max De Pree says, "The first responsibility of every leader is to define reality" (De Pree, 1998, p. 9).

Fritz's second aspect of change is to clarify the future or desired outcome—the vision. John Kotter, in *Leading Change*, defines this step as creating a vision and a strategy to direct the change effort and achieve the vision.

Fritz defines the final aspect as the movement from current reality to the future vision—the process of implementation. Kotter's parallel steps are creating a basis for action and generating short-term wins.

This perspective of change highlights the relevance of Change Styles to the effective implementation of change. The capacity to realistically and honestly portray current reality is the strength of Conservers. The capacity to imagine a new future is the strength of Originators. The capacity to find common ground and implement is the strength of Pragmatists.

The world does not lack for good ideas, only effective action and thoughtful implementation. Change, by definition, is about establishing new and different conditions, not always a positive event. Change can be accomplished effectively or ineffectively. Too often leaders, and in fact our culture, champion creativity rather than creating. They applaud a new idea and then become disillusioned when that idea has not been brought into reality. Leaders react because they do not know how to effectively implement the creative changes they seek. Effective implementation is the key to converting creativity into change.

Success Requires Working Outside Your Style

Creating change that works requires flexibility—the ability to move along the Change Style continuum, accessing and integrating all the Change Styles. When they perceive it to be necessary, Pragmatists can emulate Conservers and Originators. Conservers and Originators may act as Pragmatists, but will find it more difficult to cross the continuum to the opposite style. For all styles it is possible to operate outside of your comfort zone for short periods of time. This type of flexibility requires conscious effort and it can be exhausting. The alternative is to utilize people with different styles in a change process.

Working outside your preferred style requires deliberate attention and focus, but it can be done. Leaders have the ability to cross—or they have people who can help them cross—boundaries. This ability is crucial. The question often arises, "How do I find these people?" You already know them. Try this exercise.

Make three lists with headings of Conservers, Pragmatists and Originators. Look back at Chapter Three and review the characteristics of the three Change Styles. Think about the people with whom you work. Where do you suspect they fall? Some will be obvious. Others, such as those on the border between Conservers and Pragmatists and between Pragmatists and Originators, will be more difficult to label. Identify those people with whom you have the most conflict during times of change. These will be individuals with styles different from your own.

In groups dominated by Originators, Pragmatists may find themselves representing the Conserver perspective. In groups dominated by Conservers, Pragmatists may take on the persona of the Originator. "Those in the middle of the scale for any given group are more apt to be called upon to be flexible," says DeCiantis. "They may be stressed to do it, but they can. Again, none of us are limited by the behaviors of our preferred style. To be effective, we must be flexible."

When leaders find themselves isolated, it is a clear sign that they need to engage people with different perspectives. It is simply a matter of leaders being intentional about communicating to others in their preferred style and not expecting others to accommodate the leader's style. As you begin to put these ideas into action with the people you work with across the continuum, keep in mind these key communication strategies.

Table 2. When communicating about change with:

Conservers	Pragmatists	Originators
• Know the details • Don't start by presenting the big picture • Pick one angle and build from there • Present a minimum of information and ask what else is needed • Let them guide you with what they need to know • Ask about anticipated obstacles	• Speak in terms of outcomes • Talk about consequences of continuing down the same • Ask for recommendations for practical first steps • Ask about problems and barriers to implementation • Talk about timelines	• Think in the future • Ask what they would like to see happen • Ask for ideas • Ask about what is effective in current system (status quo) that they would not want changed • Talk about the connection between the change and future effectiveness • Give details as they are

Building Support and Commitment

People do not respect decisions made from "isolated" perspectives, nor will they support decisions made without earning commitment. In such cases, the leader directs from a position of authority and achieves only compliance, if that. As every experienced leader knows, there are two responses that will undermine efforts to lead: people who do not do what is asked of them, and those who do exactly and only what is asked of them. This latter group is sometimes the most dangerous because they let a leader's blindness to specific circumstances play itself out rather than giving input and feedback about what might work more effectively.

In the business world, when leaders create safe environments where Conservers, Pragmatists and Originators can contribute on an equal footing, outcomes are more effective. In a typical project development process, ideas come first. Someone sees a need or an opportunity and may suggest a potential solution. In that moment an idea is born and that is creativity. Other creative thinkers, typically Originators, add to ideas during this first phase of idea generation. Evaluation, another important phase of the development process has not yet begun. Evaluation is the natural strength of the Conserver. Conservers focus on details and can identify potential barriers. They look at systemic implications and can see problems that

Originators may miss. The evaluation phase is critical to any successful project, but a premature critique may prevent further exploration. Your role is to balance ideas with evaluation. If done well, implementation has more support and buy-in.

Table 3: Ideas into Action

For those acting as Pragmatists who want to create a real, tangible, positive change, the balancing of idea generation and evaluation can feel like driving down the street with one foot on the accelerator and the other on the brake. Trying to do both at the same time can be difficult, frustrating and inefficient. Pragmatists help bridge the gap in perspectives and perceptions between Originators and Conservers by building a general and collective respect for the contributions of individuals with perspectives and values all along the Change Style continuum. With that mutual respect, a group with all Change Styles represented can create the best ideas.

Two Keys to the Effective Leadership of Change

Succeeding at leadership in a dynamic world requires flexible thinking and the capacity to build relationships. The ability to see the perspective of people across the Change Style continuum is critical to successful leadership. Being able to imagine yourself in another person's position—living it and breathing it—is vital, allowing you to team with people who have the strengths you need to successfully implement tasks.

"One thing we attribute to successful leaders and artists is flexibility of mind," says DeCiantis. "Look at Leonardo da Vinci. He didn't create that many paintings, but he did a tremendous number of other things. He engaged in scientific research, conducted studies of anatomy and invented machines ahead of their time. In fact, when he died, he was in France creating war materials for King Francis I. He was successful in this broad range of interests because he kept his perceptual skills open. Pablo Picasso did the same. He would say of himself that he spent a lifetime 'becoming a child again.' He was an excellent draftsman, on par with Rembrandt in detail. He had that technique but kept himself open to new experiences and views."

We must also form relationships across the continuum. No one stands in a vacuum. "It's a myth that we do it alone, that individual creativity is it," says DeCiantis. "We need input, ideas and skills from all across the continuum. People at both ends of the spectrum must develop relationships that allow them to see how others operate. It will allow them to understand their own value and to cultivate their own flexibility."

Conclusion

DeCiantis notes that in her own work, ideas come first and are jotted down. She admits to having many books of ideas that will never be created. She also knows that if she critiques her ideas too quickly, they may be lost forever. Sometimes ideas come along ahead of their time. In fact, Leonardo da Vinci, the Fifteenth Century master of the High Renaissance, sketched out ideas for which technology did not exist to create. Jules Verne, the Nineteenth Century author of classics such as *20,000 Leagues Under the Sea* and *Around the World in Eighty Days*, wrote about capabilities that seem far less unreasonable today than when he put them to paper more than a century ago. The idea generation and evaluation process works best when we acknowledge that each is necessary for effective change and respect both perspectives because of the value that each brings.

"Each stage in the development of art is a new dialogue with a different set of materials," concludes DeCiantis. The same is true for any changing situation. Successful artists, entrepreneurs and leaders cultivate flexibility and develop relationships with people of different perspectives. Each opportunity for change requires the creation of a new dialogue with different possibilities, different risks, different players and different realities. Those leaders who can best manage that opportunity will best understand the art of change.

Notes

[1] This section is based on conversations and interviews with Cheryl DeCiantis from 1998 to 2001.

Chapter 11

HOW PEOPLE EXPERIENCE CHANGE

Transitions and Change Style Preferences

In This Chapter

The past three chapters tell stories of people planning, orchestrating, implementing and coping with complex and changing circumstances. In each story, Change Style Preferences impact perceptions of current reality, perspectives on the future, and strategies for navigating from the present into the future. This chapter:

- Explores change as a process of transition that we experience over time.
- Examines universal and predictable steps of moving through change and the implications for Change Style Preferences.
- Offers suggestions to help managers more effectively lead during times of change while avoiding behaviors that can intensify resistance to change.

It Takes Time

William Bridges, the author of *Managing Transitions,* says, "It isn't the changes that do you in, it's the transitions" (Bridges, 1991, p. 3). While change is an event—a death, birth, merger, reorganization, new job or downsizing—the human response to change is a process. Human reactions to change may include excitement, heightened emotions such as anxiety, fear and anger, and psychological trauma and confusion. So while a change is an event—a decision, a policy enacted, or a door closing unexpectedly—the psychological response is a process of transition over time. People do not typically change their attitudes, beliefs, feelings and allegiances overnight; it happens gradually.

In Search of Grace

For most of us the most profound change we can experience, then have to adjust to, is the death of a loved one. As a commonly shared experience, as well as an experience where emotions and reactions are accentuated, it provides an effective introduction to extended process of change. This is the story of Patricia's transition through the unexpected death of Grace, her healthy 17-month-old daughter (Jeffries, 2002).

Within minutes of finding her daughter not breathing, emergency medical personnel arrived. Patricia could not remember letting them in the door, but does remember the police officer looking at Grace and saying, "D.O.A." Patricia says, "I heard that and I knew what it meant, but I was still hopeful. I kept trying to revive Grace until a paramedic dragged me aside."

"For months," Patricia says, "I was angry with God. I said, 'Don't come near me, God. Don't talk to me now, God. There is nothing that you can say to me that is going to change how I feel. I just don't understand why you allowed this to happen." Patricia reports that she also tried bargaining with God. She asked him to make Grace's death a nightmare from which she could awake.

Patricia reports that, after months, she accepted her daughter's death. She is not sure exactly when this happened and she does not remember what caused it to happen. Patricia and her husband started looking for ways to ease their pain. One was to start a fund at their church to help low-income parents with children under two years of age pay for day care. They also planted a memorial garden in their yard and they converted Grace's bedroom into a guest room and made a corner of the room a special place for prayer with an alter. Some months later Patricia entered a training program at a local hospital to become a volunteer chaplain.

Today, Patricia is a volunteer chaplain. She comforts patients and their families and friends. Patricia says, "When I lift up a prayer for them, I'm praying for myself too. It's therapeutic. It's like I'm helping myself. By reaching out and helping others, you can receive healing." Patricia has formed a women's group called Motivating Grace, and the goal of the group is to help women find good things in their grief. Patricia says, "There have been so many positive things to come from her death. I knew there was something special about her. She had a purpose. God brought her into our lives for a purpose."

Patricia's story clearly portrays the range of thoughts, feelings and emotions that a person passes through as they transition from denial to acceptance, in the face of the most difficult situation most people can imagine having to face. Granted, not all of the changes in our lives are as devastating as Patricia's. But losing a job, a divorce, a business relocation or a significant shift in work patterns can generate anxiety and fear as well as grief.

The next section will examine what we have learned about the human response to change over the past 50 years.

A Brief History of Change

For over 50 years, management and organizational practitioners and theorists have speculated that personal and organizational transitions follow predictable patterns or stages, which if understood, could enable leaders to more effectively and efficiently manage organizational change. There are striking similarities in the change models of the past half-century. For example, each model describes similar, predictable and sequential cognitive and emotional reactions. However, none of the models address the impact of our personalities and personal preferences as we pass through these stages of transition. The consequence of ignoring personality preferences is a "one size fits all" management style that really does not facilitate effective change.

Understanding the relationship between Change Style Preference and the predictable reactions we experience as we pass through a change event can make us better managers during times of transition. This translates into less resistance, quicker engagement and higher commitment within teams.

Wouldn't it be great to have a predictable process to help you better understand and manage individuals and teams as they experience change? You're in luck. We have developed one based on 50 years of theory and research.

1947

Kurt Lewin described the process of change as occurring in three stages: Unfreezing, Moving, and Refreezing (Weisbord, 1987, pp. 226-227). These labels describe the sequential process through which existing systems are undone, rearranged and reconstituted. Lewin's model describes the cognitive, as well as emotional, response of individuals to change. First, individuals must recognize that the "old system or state" is history and reduce their attachment to doing things in a familiar way. This Unfreezing stage challenges the status quo with different and maybe discomforting information. In the second stage—Moving—new ideas, structures and systems are created, tested and installed to replace those that existed previously. In the third stage—Refreezing—the new systems are accepted, refined and operated to produce results.

Table 4. A Brief History of Change

1947 — Lewin

1. Unfreezing	2. Moving	3. Refreezing
Triggered by social problem or conflict Anxiety Fear Unconscious behaviors	Changing values, attitudes, structure, feelings, behaviors Uncertainty Excitement	New support mechanisms New perspectives New status quo New identity

1969 — Kubler-Ross

1. Denial & Isolation	2. Anger 3. Bargaining 4. Depression	5. Acceptance
Believe life is as it was before our loss Reenact rituals Flashbacks to past experiences	Blame others or ourselves for our loss Easily agitated, emotional outbursts Making deals with ourselves or with God Feeling listless and tired Feeling guilty Feelings of being punished	For dying: Resignation, withdrawal, lack of emotion For survivors: Realization that life has to go on, acceptance of loss, new focus on future goals and activities, renewed energy

1980 — Bridges

1. Letting Go	2. Neutral Zone	3. New Beginnings
Sadness Frightened Depressed Grieving	High anxiety Lower motivation Self-doubt Lower energy Disoriented Polarization Lost Confused Uncertain	New understanding New values New attitudes New identities Finality of past Risk Pressure Accountability Stress

1982 — Janssen

1. Denial	2. Confusion	3. Renewal	4. Contentment
Lack of awareness Fear of change Insensitive to events	Out of touch Scattered Unsure Different	Sincere Open Exploring Willing to risk	Satisfied Calm Realistic Like the status quo

1988 — Scott & Jaffe

1. Denial	2. Resistance	3. Exploration	4. Commitment
Focused on past Neglecting future Lack of awareness Nothing happens Work as usual Turn a blind eye Productivity decreases Numbness	Self-doubt Depression Anxiety Frustration Fear Uncertainty Drastic productivity dips Accidents increase Sickness increases	Internal creative energy increases Excitement Exhilarating New bonds created Chaotic Everything in question Stress & uncertainty Searching Testing Experimenting	New roles New applications Refocus on a plan Solid identification Clear expectations Clear goals Clear direction

1990 — Spencer & Adams

1. Losing Focus 2. Minimizing Impact	3. The Pit	4. Letting Go 5. Testing Limits	6. Search for Meaning 7. Full Integration
Sense of confusion Denial Act as if everything is normal Put on a happy face	Most difficult and painful stage Feeling of sadness, anger and fear	Focus on opportunities & creating a new future Releasing energy Increased optimism, enthusiasm & vitality	A sense of mastery Improved self-esteem The change is now a part of your life

1969

Elisabeth Kubler-Ross, a Swiss-born psychiatrist, is one of the world's most respected authorities on grief. In 1969 she published her seminal work on the topic, *On Death and Dying*. In this book she outlined five commonly experienced stages for those facing death or experiencing the death of a loved one. These stages include Denial and Isolation, Anger, Bargaining, Depression and Acceptance. Denial is a temporary defense mechanism. As the word implies, Denial involves activities and rituals that are reflective of life before the change occurred. In this stage, people refuse to believe what has happened. Stage 2 is Anger. In this stage, Denial is replaced by feelings of anger, rage, envy, and resentment. A common question is: "Why me?" The third stage is Bargaining. Bargains are typically made with God and are attempts to postpone the inevitable. Kubler-Ross's fourth stage is Depression. Depression has two aspects. The first is related to losses in the past, such as living at home, a job or the ability to care for loved ones. The second aspect of Depression is related to losses in the future. In the final stage of grief, Acceptance, an individual accepts the inevitable. Kubler-Ross describes Acceptance by the dying person not as a happy time but rather a time that is almost devoid of feeling. For survivors, this is the time when they realize that life must go on; the loss is accepted and attention is turned toward the future. While Kubler-Ross's grief model focuses on significant individual loss, it has been applied extensively to workplace losses such as jobs. Kubler-Ross's work has provided the theoretical foundation for much of the work of Hospice.

1980

In his earlier book, *Transitions*, William Bridges developed a three-stage transition model similar to Lewin's. Bridges' transition model includes Letting Go, the Neutral Zone, and New Beginnings. The first stage, Letting Go, recognizes the end of something and acknowledges the experience of loss. The second stage, the Neutral Zone, is described as a "no man's land" that exists between the old and new realities. Bridges calls this the Neutral Zone because "it is a nowhere between two somewheres" (Bridges, 1980, p. 35). The Neutral Zone is a broad category incorporating the negative emotions of resistance and the more positive emotions associated with exploration and new possibilities. People operating in this zone feel uncomfortable and emotionally awkward as they confront the unfamiliar and unknown. In this stage, both danger and opportunity exist. Some people may persevere and others may abandon the situation. Only after organizations experience Letting Go and the Neutral Zone can they begin the third stage, New Beginnings.

1982

Claes Janssen, a social psychologist, presented a four-stage model for explaining the process of change. In *Productive Workplaces*, Weisbord (1987, pp. 266-268) summarizes Janssen's model. The four stages in Janssen's model include Denial, Confusion, Renewal and Contentment. In the first stage, Denial, individuals have difficulty recognizing or acknowledging that a change is taking place and, if they do, they are at least partially disconnected from their emotions. In Stage 2, Confusion, individuals acknowledge the change but may resist it. Fear, uncertainty and anger are typical emotions in this stage with rumors abounding and people speculating about the future. Stage 3, Renewal, occurs when individuals begin to accept the change and are willing to take risks to explore and create new and different situations for themselves. Contentment—Stage 4—is achieved when individuals are aligned with the new order and are accepting of future prospects. With the new order becoming the new status quo, individuals are satisfied and calm.

1988

Cynthia Scott and Dennis Jaffe also created a widely used four-stage change process model which was originally published in the *Training and Development Journal.* The Scott-Jaffe model incorporated the work of Dr. Elisabeth Kubler-Ross on death and grieving with their own observations of behaviors during mergers, downsizing and closures. They also labeled the first stage of their model Denial. During the Denial stage, either awareness of the change or the true meaning of the change has not yet been recognized. While in Denial, you are in cognitive disbelief and/or are emotionally disconnected. Denial has to be overcome before the next stage of transition can occur. Stage 2, Resistance, begins when people acknowledge the change, but do not necessarily accept it. In Resistance, people experience doubt, anger, disbelief and fear. Stage 3, Exploring, involves looking forward and considering ways to participate in the emerging future. During Exploration, individuals become more open to new possibilities and start to investigate options and opportunities. In Stage 4, Commitment, individuals become committed to the new situation and have a reasonable level of comfort with their new roles and responsibilities. The change is successfully completed when the organization produces satisfactory results again.

1990

In 1990, Sabrina Spencer and John Adams published *Life Changes: Growing Through Personal Transitions.* In this work, Spencer and Adams described seven stages that define the nature of personal transition. As with Kubler-Ross, theirs is not limited to organizational transitions, but focuses more on personal transitions that may or may not be work-related. The first two stages, Losing Focus and Minimizing Impact, describe a sense of confusion and disorientation followed by denial and attempts to act as if nothing has changed. Stage 3, The Pit, is the most difficult and painful stage. It includes feelings of sadness, anger and fear. The next two stages, Letting Go and Testing Limits, include a shift from the past to the future. In Letting Go there is a focus on opportunities and possibilities. With Testing Limits comes a release of energy, along with increased optimism, enthusiasm and vitality. The last two stages, Search for Meaning and Full Integration, bring a sense of confidence in ability to manage the future. Self-esteem increases and with this comes an increase in satisfaction. With Full Integration comes the completion of the change. The change is no longer a "thing" that is happening to you but rather a part of your new life.

A New Model: Stages of Transition

There is a lot of overlap among the six theories, whether they contain three, four, five or seven stages. The stages in each of the models present a common and predictable pattern. Our model, Stages of Transition, refers to these stages as 1) Acknowledging, 2) Reacting, 3) Investigating and 4) Implementing.

Table 5. Stages of Transition

Past ⟶			Future
Lewin	Unfreezing	Moving	Refreezing
Kubler-Ross	Denial	Anger/Bargaining/ Depression	Acceptance
Bridges	Letting Go	Neutral Zone	New Beginnings
Janssen	Denial	Confusion	Renewal	Contentment
Scott & Jaffe	Denial	Resistance	Exploration	Commitment
Spencer & Adams	Losing Focus/ Minimizing Impact	The Pit	Letting Go/ Testing Limits	Sense of Meaning/Full Integration
Stages of Transition	Stage 1 Acknowledging	Stage 2 Reacting	Stage 3 Investigating	Stage 4 Implementing

Reacting and Investigating represent the most challenging parts of any change process. This is where perspective shifts from old to new and where most emotional energy is expended.

This part of the change process offers the greatest challenges and opportunities. This is where change can be directed, facilitated and managed. It is also in these stages that most change efforts are either derailed or significantly impaired.

Table 6. Stages of Transition Summary—Typical Reactions

Stage 1: Acknowledging	• People are shocked and feel threatened. • People deny that a change has happened. • People appear slower in their thinking, distracted, and forgetful. Example: Productivity is low.
Stage 2: Reacting	• People express various reactions—anger, depression, withdrawal, etc. • People try to "bargain" to do things the "old" way. • People believe they can "wait out" the change and everything will return to normal. • People recycle back to Stage 1 when their emotions are denied or ignored.
Stage 3: Investigating	• People may express grief/sadness over loss, but they begin to explore the possibility of future options. • People may mix a willingness to explore new options with reservation. • Emotions can range from excitement to anxiety.
Stage 4: Implementing	• People appear ready to establish new routines, adapt to new systems, and help others learn new ways. • People's comfort with the change engenders more flexibility, creativity and risk taking on the job. • The change is not viewed as a "change" but "the way we do things around here."

No Pain, No Gain

Most change initiatives want people to jump in at the stages of investigating and implementing, thus avoiding the messier and frequently more negative part of transition—reacting. Reacting, in particular, is seen as undesirable or unnecessary. In practice, change efforts are often prolonged by well-intended, but uninformed, efforts to move straight to the latter stages of transition. Planners and organizers of change forget that through the planning process they have already experienced their own denial and resistance and thus are ahead of the troops in the transition curve. Among their teams, commitment to new beginnings comes only after they have traveled the transitory path from denial to confusion and resistance, and then to exploration and renewal.

A Holistic Approach

From the four models an integrated model emerges that reflects the common patterns, experiences and insights gained from each body of work. This model identifies four stages of transition: Acknowledging, Reacting, Investigating and Implementing. Effective and ineffective behaviors can be defined for each of the stages. The bottom line is that each of the four stages is predictable, normal and, in fact, can bring value to a change initiative. So the model describes and explains change-related behaviors and it suggests actions that can be taken to improve the management of change initiatives.

Discovery Learning® Change Process Model

Discovery Learning® Change Process Model

Cognitive Domain

Change Event

I Acknowledging   IV Implementing

Past Orientation   Future Orientation

Reacting   Investigating

II   III

Emotional Domain

Not One but Two Transitions

This Change Process Model actually involves two transitions. The first transition involves our orientation in time as we move from a focus on the past to a focus on the future. The second transition is a shift from experiencing our situation from a more cognitive orientation (rational and analytical) to a more emotional orientation and then back again to the more cognitive orientation.

Past to future tracks our orientation with regard to time. In the "past" orientation, attention is primarily on systems, policies, loyalties and procedures that have been in place historically and leading up to the change event. The "future" orientation is toward emerging systems, procedures and opportunities. The transition from past to future orientation (Reacting to Investigating) is a critical time in any transition process. This transition is more likely to be gradual, with attention shifting back and forth from past to future rather than being abrupt and final. Characteristic of this transition is a shift from negative emotions such as anger, resentment and anxiety to more positive emotions such as acceptance, excitement and curiosity.

Our **cognitive vs. emotional** orientation impacts the way we solve problems and make decisions. On the cognitive side, we work more from a logical and analytical orientation. On the emotional side, our feelings may supersede our logic and rationality. Everyone operates from each of these domains and some people clearly prefer one to the other. This is similar to the thinking/feeling preference identified by Carl Jung and popularized in the work of Myers and Briggs. Whatever our normal preference for thinking or feeling, there are times when people decide and respond more out of their cognitive capacity and times when they are more likely to be more emotional. In the stages of Acknowledging and Implementing, the tendency is for us to operate from our logic, while in Reacting we tend to operate more from our emotions. The stage of Investigating typically starts from an emotional orientation and as we transition from this stage to Implementing we also transition toward our logical and more rational orientation.

Any significant change process includes a jumble of beliefs, behaviors and emotions. While it is easiest to focus on the behaviors, leaders should not forget that deeply held beliefs, conscious or unconscious, drive the emotions and consequently the behaviors of individuals experiencing change. One of the tenets of good "emotional intelligence" is that actions are taken with an awareness of how the actions are influenced by emotions. While this is a perspective rooted in cognitive psychology, it is not intended to diminish the reality or significance of emotional reactions. Rather, the intention is to understand the behavior, yours and others, within the context of emotions that are both predictable and normal.

Transition and Change Style Preferences

Whether Conservers, Pragmatists or Originators, we have natural strengths as well as potential traps during each of the stages of transition. Being aware of these can enable us to manage our reactions as well as our response to change. Understanding these strengths and traps can also help us to better help others during times of change.

Table 7. Transitions and Change Style Preferences

Stage 1: Acknowledging	Strengths	Potential Traps
Conservers	• For mild or moderate change, acknowledging the current reality of existing systems/situations and transitioning into the Reacting Stage	• When ready for the Reacting Stage, showing a lack of patience with those in denial
Pragmatists	• Being patient and understanding	• Having trouble boldly presenting difficult information
Originators	• For drastic change, quickly acknowledging the new reality and moving into the Reacting Stage	• Difficulty acknowledging the value and legitimacy of current reality

Stage 2: Reacting	Strengths	Potential Traps
Conservers	• Thoroughly exploring the long-range consequences of a change	• Staying in this stage longer than other Change Styles
Pragmatists	• Assisting with communication between those in resistance and in investigating	• Vacillating between Reacting and Investigating • Avoiding conflict
Originators	• Passing through this stage with little resistance or expressed emotion	• Passing through this stage without considering critical, long-term consequences of the change • Being impatient with people in the Reacting Stage

Stage 3: Investigating	Strengths	Potential Traps
Conservers	• Focusing upon realistic possibilities	• Moving quickly to implementation without exploring options
Pragmatists	• Weighing pros and cons of various options	• Vacillating between Reacting and Investigating
Originators	• Openness to exploring • Seeing possibilities and potential	• Feeling comfortable in this stage and not wanting to move to implementation

Stage 4: Implementing	Strengths	Potential Traps
Conservers	• Putting new systems and procedures in place • Making improvements over time	• Defining the new systems and procedures before there is time for input from others • Becoming comfortable with the status quo
Pragmatists	• Focusing energy to get the ball rolling • Involving others in the implementation process • Team building	• Over-focusing on making everyone happy
Originators	• Communicating and reinforcing the vision	• Lack of follow-through • Loss of interest in the project • Not enough attention to daily operations

By exploring Change Style Preferences in conjunction with this model, you can improve prospects for effective change by integrating predictable responses to change (yours and those of others) with strategies that can help organizations successfully navigate change. This is the topic of the next chapter.

Transition and Change Style Traps

When faced with major transitions nearly everyone will experience the four stages of transition. Some people move through stages faster or slower than others. The speed of transition is impacted by two key factors: the degree of emotional and psychological threat posed by the change and the person's change style preference.

The Conserver Trap

Conservers are convergent thinkers and are most likely to spend more time in reacting than the other two change styles. Convergent thinkers will ask more detailed questions about the reasons for the change as well as the consequences of the change. When they do not receive adequate answers to their questions they become more concerned and uncertain about the change. Since the Reacting stage of transition is more laden with emotions related to uncertainty, Conservers will often appear fearful or anxious. The more their fears and anxieties are ignored or minimized the more resistant they are likely to become. The manner in which Conservers are led while they are in the Reacting Stage of transition will result in them either moving on to Investigating or becoming resistors of the change.

Once a Conserver moves through Reacting they will quickly move to the Implementing phase of the transition. Conservers usually spend little time in Investigating. Investigating involves divergent exploration of options and possibilities. Conservers, in general, do not want a lot of options to select form. They prefer one or two good choices from which they will make a fairly quick decision and then they are ready to implement.

The Pragmatist Trap

Pragmatists are bridgers and consensus builders. The Pragmatist trap tends to occur at the transition point from Reacting to Investigating. Pragmatists often feel torn between Reacting and Investigating. They describe the tension between trying to slow down the Originators who are racing into Investigating and pulling along the Conservers who are imbedded in Reacting. Their need for 100% buy in from all stakeholders and their desire to have all stakeholders in the same space adds to their sense of suspension between Reacting and Investigating.

The Originator Trap

As much as Conservers are convergent thinkers, Originators are divergent thinkers. They are in their element when they are exploring options and possibilities. Every problem can be expanded to see multiple tangentially related issues. Since Originators enjoy exploring possibilities they are attracted to the Investigating phase of transition. Consequently, they move quickly through Reacting. This is especially true when the Originator generates or at least controls the change. The Reacting phase may pose more challenge to Originators when they are in situations where they lack control.

Since Originators like exploration and divergent thinking they may become trapped in the Investigating phase of transition. It may become challenging for the Originator to let go of multiple options and converge on one final choice. The result is that Originators may have trouble moving from Investigating to Implementing.

If the ultimate goal is to move into the Implementation phase of the transition then the Conservers may get there as quickly as the Originators. They will be delayed in different phases of transition which may look and feel really different to the people trying to lead them. The way the different change styles are led through the four phases of transition will have a significant impact on whether they successfully arrive at the final phase of Implementation.

Chapter 12

LEADING CHANGE EFFECTIVELY

Using What You've Learned to Lead Change

In This Chapter

This chapter will show you how to use the information we have explored thus far—Change Style Preferences and the Stages of Transition—to become a more effective leader of change. We will provide:

- The primary leadership imperatives for each stage of transition.
- The do's and don'ts for leading effectively in each of the stages of transition.
- Change Style Preference strengths and problems at each of the transition stages.
- Suggestions for effective behavior for Conservers, Pragmatists and Originators at the most problematic stages in the change transition process.

- A checklist for leading your next change initiative, large or small.

The Leadership Imperatives

The requirements for effective leadership change as people progress through the stages of transition. To acknowledge change, people need information. Information should be given honestly, factually and with compassion. Often the information needs to be heard multiple times before it is understood and/or believed. This also requires patience.

When reacting to change, people need support. Their emotions must be acknowledged, accepted and respected. This does not imply agreement, but does require honest listening and sympathy.

When people begin to enter the Investigating stage of transition, the leadership imperative becomes to provide encouragement. People need encouragement to explore new possibilities and potential benefits of the change.

As people enter the last stage of transition, Implementing, the leadership imperative becomes reinforcement. People are actively implementing new ideas, systems and projects, and need reinforcement for their initiative and successes.

The following table outlines the leadership imperative for each stage of transition along with suggestions for behaviors leaders should engage in, as well as avoid.

Table 8. Leading People in Transition

	Do's	Don'ts
ACKNOWLEDGING **Leadership Imperative:** *GIVE* *INFORMATION*	• Give visible support & provide information consistently & repeatedly • Provide facts • Assist with support networks	• Hit people over the head with the truth • Push for acknowledgement (this intensifies denial)
REACTING **Leadership Imperative:** *GIVE* *SUPPORT*	• Listen • Acknowledge the feelings of those in resistance • Provide time (as the situation allows) • Provide facts • Be empathetic • Identify areas of stability	• Argue • Provide reasons why they should not feel the way they feel • Convince them this is good for them • Push exploration (this can result in movement back to denial)
INVESTIGATING **Leadership Imperative:** *GIVE* *ENCOURAGEMENT*	• Create opportunities to explore new possibilities • Reward exploration • Employ participative decision making • Outline pros and cons of new possibilities	• Push choices • Rush choices • Punish mistakes • Overestimate or misrepresent future options
IMPLEMENTING **Leadership Imperative:** *GIVE* *REINFORCEMENT*	• Clarify desired outcomes • Reward effective performance • Support risk taking & innovation • Encourage communication • Get out of the way	• Micro-manage • Control choices • Limit participation

The Discovery Learning Change Process Model presented in Chapter Eleven is shown again below with the leadership imperatives imbedded in the model.

Figure 2. Leadership Imperatives

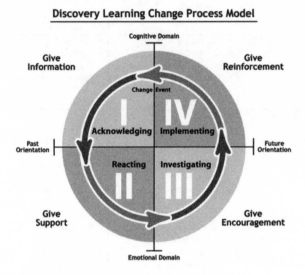

Stage 1: Acknowledging

This stage of transition begins as soon as a change occurs or is announced. This stage is primarily a cognitive process involving acknowledgment of the event. Denial, both cognitive and emotional, is common in this stage. After learning of a significant change, especially one with negative implications, people may proceed as if they had not heard. This is cognitive denial. On the other hand, someone may show evidence that they are aware of the change but demonstrate no emotional response. They are matter-of-fact and show little or no emotional reaction. This is emotional denial.

The terrorist attacks on the United States on September 11, 2001, provided many examples of both cognitive and emotional denial. Even days after seeing the planes crash into the World Trade Center towers, people reported thinking they would wake and discover that they were dreaming. On an emotional level, over a week after the disaster, relatives of some victims reported that they remained optimistic that their loved ones would be found alive. New York City mayor Rudolf Gulliani strategically and sensitively communicated the diminishing probability of finding survivors after it was nearly certain that no survivors would be found.

Even for people who experienced no direct personal loss in the September 11 attacks, there was a reaction of disbelief. For days people repeatedly watched television replays of the planes crashing into the towers and the towers tumbling down. For many people this repeated viewing of the disaster seemed necessary for the event to become more real and less like a dream or movie.

A career counselor described a man who, after losing his job in a downsizing, would get up each morning, put on his suit, go to his old office and sit in the lobby. It took him three weeks to tell his wife he had lost his job. Events that are unexpected, even those with the potential for positive impact, can take time to assimilate into our cognition. When the event is beyond our ability to imagine, the denial becomes more exaggerated.

Effective Leadership

Effective leadership in the Acknowledging stage of the transition process involves assessing the level of denial and providing information. Information should be provided clearly, honestly, compassionately and consistently. The information should be delivered by the leader and not delegated to others. Delivery of information by someone who is perceived to be important intensifies awareness of the message.

Stage 2: Reacting

Once individuals gain cognitive and emotional awareness of the change, they transition into the second phase of the change process, Reacting. This stage typically reflects strong emotions including anger, withdrawal, depression and resistance. People may actively attempt to regain or retain past policies, duties and relationships.

Many change strategists would prefer to skip this step and begin with Investigation and Exploration. When Reacting is not accepted as a natural and valuable component of change, resistance intensifies and, as a consequence, this stage becomes the overriding focus of many change efforts. People are labeled as resistors and strategies for dealing with resistors are debated, crafted and implemented.

Reacting and resisting are natural and valuable parts of any change process. There are tough questions that need to be asked and answered. Why do we need to do this? How will this make us better? Have you thought about the consequences of this change for . . . ? Have we thought about the system implications regarding coordination and integration?

It is in this stage of the change process that Change Style Preferences become most pronounced. People with a Conserver orientation may find it more challenging to shift from a past to a future orientation, thus remaining in the Reacting stage longer. Those with an Originator orientation may pass through this stage quickly, moving to Investigating or future orientation. As a result, Stage 2 could be problematic for both strong Conservers and Originators. Originators may buy into the change so quickly that they fail to thoroughly consider the implications for work, organizational and human systems. While Conservers are asking the tough questions that need to be addressed, their challenge is to not get stuck and become negative if they perceive their concerns are not being heard or are discounted.

Effective Leadership

Effective leadership during the Reacting Stage involves listening. People need to feel heard even if you cannot agree. Ignoring, arguing with and discounting the perspectives of others will only serve to increase resistance and will not win people over. In fact, negative and aggressive behavior by management as people transition into this stage may even result in a slide back into denial. Listening should be sincere and the listener should remain open to the possibility of gaining useful information for directing the change process. Effective leadership also includes bridging between people already in Investigating and those still in Reacting. This requires real flexibility which is typically the strength of Pragmatists.

Stage 3: Investigating

The movement into this phase marks a transition from a past orientation to a future orientation. Generally, the transition will not be clean and immediate. A gradual shift with back-and-forth movement is more typical. As time passes, more time is spent focusing on the future. People begin to accept change on an emotional level and become more open to future possibilities. A slight willingness to consider future opportunities can evolve into full-blown excitement and enthusiasm about new possibilities. This stage can result in a mixture of emotions from excitement about new possibilities to anxiety and fear of the unknown.

Effective Leadership

Effective leadership in the Investigating stage looks for and acknowledges evidence of this shift and creates awareness of new opportunities to encourage exploration. However, it is important to be realistic and honest about what is possible. Whether intentional or not, the perception of dishonesty in superiors can easily push people from exploration back into resistance.

Originators are most comfortable in the Investigating stage. Originators tend to move quickly through Reacting to reach this stage, but then may find it challenging to move beyond Investigating into the final stage of Implementing. In terms of

Myers-Briggs terminology, Originators are characteristically Perceivers. This means they like to explore possibilities and keep their options open as long as they can. The final stage of Implementing is not their strong suit.

Stage 4: Implementing

In the final stage of the Change Process Model, new options have been examined and decisions made. People are now ready to begin the process of implementing new jobs and responsibilities. During this stage, people settle into a new routine. They develop a level of comfort and familiarity with responsibilities and also begin the process of improvement and refinement. This is the domain of the Conserver and the Pragmatist.

The transition from Investigating to Implementing marks the transition from a more emotional orientation to a more cognitive orientation. Typically less emotion will be visible. At this stage people will have adjusted to the change or will have moved on to a more suitable setting.

Effective Leadership

Effective leadership in the Implementing stage will set clear goals, objectives, standards and expectations. They will reinforce effective behavior and outcomes and provide effective and timely feedback when needed. Effective leadership will also seek out and encourage constant fine-tuning of the current operating systems as well as ideas for innovation and rejuvenation.

Bringing It All Together

Effective change is about creating. It takes an organization working together with multiple perspectives to bring about effective changes. Effective Conservers best understand current reality and know what must be salvaged (i.e., what's working and what is not). Effective Conservers can ensure that the baby is not thrown out with the bathwater. Effective Originators can envision new opportunities and can imagine new possibilities. They live in the future. They encourage movement away from the status quo. Effective Pragmatists can bring these two groups together and incorporate their collective views into a plan that will move the organization forward. It takes all these perspectives working together to create and manage the "creative tension" between the current situation and new possibilities that Fritz, in *The Path of Least Resistance,* calls the engine that brings about change.

The same creative tension that brings about change in an organization can be created within an individual leader. To be effective, a leader must learn to balance and integrate all the different change perspectives, knowing when to allow each to dominate. To do this you must know yourself, understand others and understand the predictable reaction and responses that any significant change will elicit. Ideas are only a starting point. Although ideas are essential, and those who are good at coming up with ideas are useful to the organization, it requires a team of people uniting perspectives, talents and energy to bring an idea into existence. Creativity is only the beginning point on the path to creating.

Now it's time to consider how you can use what you've learned to your best advantage. The following worksheet is designed to help you apply what you've learned the next time you are faced with a change process—large or small, at home or at work, as a leader or as a participant.

Appendix

Effectively Managing Change Worksheet

Define the change effort and your role in it.

What are the organization's expectations of this change effort?

What are your expectations of this change effort?

For this change effort what concerns will be raised by:

Conservers	Pragmatists	Originators
_____	_____	_____
_____	_____	_____
_____	_____	_____
_____	_____	_____
_____	_____	_____
_____	_____	_____
_____	_____	_____
_____	_____	_____

How can you assists each of the Change Styles with these concerns?

Conservers	Pragmatists	Originators

For the key stakeholders who do you think typifies each of these Change Styles?

Conservers	Pragmatists	Originators

For this change effort what strengths do each of the Change Styles bring?

Conservers	Pragmatists	Originators

What specific contributions and challenges can each involved person make to the change effort?

Name _____

Contributions   Challenges

_____   _____
_____   _____
_____   _____
_____   _____

Name _____

Contributions   Challenges

_____   _____
_____   _____
_____   _____
_____   _____

Name _____

Contributions   Challenges

_____   _____
_____   _____
_____   _____
_____   _____

Name _____

Contributions   Challenges

_____   _____
_____   _____
_____   _____
_____   _____

What are your unique contributions and challenges?

Contributions   Challenges

_____   _____
_____   _____
_____   _____
_____   _____
_____   _____
_____   _____
_____   _____

What actions can you take to assist people in each stage of transition?

Acknowledging: _____
_____
_____
_____

Reacting: _____
_____
_____
_____

Investigating: _____
_____
_____
_____

Implementing: _____
_____
_____
_____

References

Argyris, Chris (1982). *Reasoning, Learning and Action: Individual and Organizational,* San Francisco: Jossey-Bass.

Boukreev, Anatoli and G. Watson DeWalt, (1977). *The Climb,* St. Martin Press.

Breashears, David (1999). *High Exposure,* Touchstone Books.

Bridges, William (1980). *Transitions,* Reading, MA: Addison-Wesley Publishing.

Bridges, William (1991). *Managing Transition,* Reading, MA: Addison-Wesley Publishing.

Bronstad, Amanda (1999). "Lawsuit Filed on Drkoop Options," *Austin Business Journal,* Nov. 19, Vol. 19, Issue 37.

Bronstad, Amanda (2000). "DrKoop.com's New CEO Weighs Options for Future," *Washington Business Journal,* Sept. 15, Vol. 19, Issue 19.

Carrns, Ann (2000). "Charting One Internet Patient's Rapid Decline," *Wall Street Journal,* April 6.

Charatan, Fred (1999). "DrKoop.com Criticized for Mixing Information with Advertising," *BMJ: British Medical Journal,* Sept. 18, Issue 7212.

De Pree, Max (1998). *The Art of Leadership,* New York: Doubleday.

"DrKoop.com Prospects Dim," *Inter@ctive Week*, August 14, Volume 7, Issue 32.

Fritz, Robert (1989). *The Path of Least Resistance*, New York: Fawcett-Clumbine.

Fryer, Bronwyn (2001). "Leading Through Rough Times: An Interview with Novell's Eric Schmidt," *Harvard Business Review*, May, Volume 79, Number 5.

Hamel, Gary (2001). "Revolution vs. Evolution: You Need Both," *Harvard Business Review*, May, Volume 79, Number 5.

Janssen, Claes (1982). *Personlig Dialektik* (2nd ed.), Stockholm: Liber.

Jeffries, Cynthia (2002). "A Search for Grace," *The News and Record*, Greensboro, NC, March 31.

Kotter, John (1996). *Leading Change*, Boston: Harvard Business School Press Publishing.

Krakauer, Jon (1999). *Into Thin Air*, Anchor Books.

Kubler-Ross, Elisabeth (1969). *On Death and Dying*, New York: Simon & Schuster.

Musselwhite, Christopher (1999). *Change Style Indicator Facilitator Guide*, Discovery Learning Press.

Musselwhite, Christopher (2000). *Change Style Indicator Research and Development Report*, Discovery Learning Press.

Nasri, Jennifer (2000). "Dot-Coms Forced to Lay Off Employees in Attempt to Make a Profit," *Weekly Corporate Growth Report*, June 26, Issue 1098.

Sarudi, Dagmara (2000). "Drkoop Plunge Bodes Ill for B-to-C Firms," *H&HN:—Hospitals & Health Networks*, May, Vol. 74, Issue 5.

Schibsted, Evantheia (1999). "Consulting Dr. Koop's Medical Record," *Forbes*, Vol. 164, Issue 4.

Schwartz, Nelson D. & Margaret Boitano (2000). "Dr. Koop and the Greed Disease," *Fortune*, May 29, Vol. 141, Issue 11.

"Scoop: Hang' with Dr. Koop," *Brandweek*, Nov. 11, 1999, Vol. 40, Issue 2.

Scott, Cynthia D. & Dennis T. Jaffe (1988). "Survive and Thrive in Times of Change," *Training and Development Journal*, April.

Senge, Peter (1990). *The Fifth Discipline: The Art and Practice of the Learning Organization*, Doubleday Currency: New York.

Sherrid, Pamela (1999). "What's Up, Dr. Koop?" *U.S. News & World Report*, Sept. 20, Vol. 127, Issue 11.

Spencer, Sabina & John Adams (1990). *Life Changes: Growing Through Personal Transitions*, San Francisco, CA: Self-published, johndadams@worldnet.att.net.

Stoneham, Laurie (1999). "Koop Lends His Name to Online Medical Info," *Austin Business Journal*, April 23, Vol. 19, Issue 8.

Weisbord, Marvin (1987). *Productive Workplaces*, San Francisco: Jossey-Bass Publishers.

Wetlaufer, Suzy (2001). "The Business Case Against Revolution: An Interview with Nestlé's Peter Brabeck," *Harvard Business Review*, February, Volume 79, Number 2.

About the Authors

Christopher Musselwhite

Christopher Musselwhite founded Discovery Learning in 1990. He is currently the president and CEO. The organization has a broad range of international expertise in human resource and organizational development. Chris has been involved in organizational and human resource development since 1972 and has held a variety of positions including associate professor of engineering and industrial management, and senior adjunct program associate at the Center for Creative Leadership.

With a degree in product design and a master's degree in industrial engineering, Chris received the Ed.D. in Adult Learning from North Carolina State University in 1985, with an emphasis in management and organizational development. He has published numerous articles and four book chapters on leadership development, manufacturing management, self-managed teams and time-based innovation. Chris and Discovery Learning products have been featured in *BusinessWeek, InfoWorld, Training and Development Journal, Work Force Training News, Training, Successful Meetings Magazine, Enterprise, BusinessWeek Japan* and *Fortune.*

Randell Jones

Randell Jones is a communications and leadership development consultant and an award-winning author. He has researched and written articles for Excursions, Discovery Learning's quarterly newsletter.

For nearly a decade, he consulted for a national employee benefits firm where he managed the communications division. He has project experience in a variety of settings including engineering, manufacturing, trucking, hospitals, textiles, banking, nonprofits, tourism, and state and local government.

Prior to undertaking his current career, Randell worked eight years as a water resources engineer and earned his professional engineer license. He holds bachelor and master's degrees in engineering from Georgia Tech and earned his MBA from UNC-Chapel Hill.